Getting Started in

Tax-Savvy Investing

The Getting Started In Series

Getting Started in
Tax-Savvy Investing

Andrew Westhem
Don Korn

A Marketplace Book

John Wiley & Sons, Inc.

New York • Chichester • Weinheim • Brisbane • Singapore • Toronto

Published by John Wiley & Sons, Inc.

Published simultaneously in Canada.

This publication is designed to provide accurate and authoritative information in regard to the subject matter covered. It is sold with the understanding that the publisher is not engaged in rendering legal, accounting, or other professional services. If legal advice or other expert assistance is required, the services of a competent professional person should be sought.

Designations used by companies to distinguish their products are often claimed as trademarks. In all instances where the author or publisher is aware of a claim, the product names appear in Initial Capital letters. Readers, however, should contact the appropriate companies for more complete information regarding trademarks and registration.

Library of Congress Cataloging-in-Publication Data:

Westhem, Andrew D., 1933–
 Getting started in tax-savvy investing / Andrew Westhem, Don Korn.
  p. cm.—(The getting started in)
 Includes index.
 ISBN 0-471-36330-8 (paper : acid-free paper)
 1. Investments—Taxation—United States. 2. Tax shelters—United States. 3. Tax planning—United States. I. Korn, Donald Jay. II. Title. III. Series.
HG4910.W3838 2000
 336.24'24—dc21   99-055546

Printed in the United States of America

10 9 8 7 6 5 4 3 2 1

This book is dedicated to you the reader.
By making the decision to buy our book, you've
taken the first step to educating yourself
about tax-savvy investing. We trust you'll
find this investment to be extremely
rewarding, before- and after-tax.

Contents

Introduction

Despite all the articles about "tax cuts" and "tax relief," the truth is that Americans are paying taxes at much higher levels than historically has been the case. Our political system virtually dictates this result.

After all, tax laws are passed by Congress and signed by Presidents: politicians all. Their main goal is reelection; in order to attain this goal they need enormous amounts of money. That's why politicians are always out raising funds.

Where do most of those funds come from? From special interest groups, big corporations, and wealthy families. Those generous donors all want something in return: tax breaks.

BANKING ON BREAKS

As a result, the U.S. tax code is filled with tax deductions, tax exemptions, and tax credits. Many of these tax breaks have been around for so long they're now taken for granted.

For example, if you own a home you can deduct the interest on your mortgage. Everybody knows that; it's as natural as the sun rising in the east.

In truth, though, the United States is the only major nation with deductible mortgage interest (such interest may be partially deductible in the United Kingdom) and this deduction has a relatively brief history. Back in the Depression of the 1930s, President Franklin Roosevelt pushed through this deduction to help the real estate interests that had supported his campaign.

HOW THE RICH GET RICHER

As you might expect, many tax code loopholes are intended to benefit wealthy families, who want to minimize gift and estate taxes as well as income taxes. Ever since the tax code was overhauled in 1913, wealthy families have had their lawyers and accountants working on ways to hold down their tax bills.

Until now, many of those techniques were closely held secrets. In this book, though, we're breaking the code of silence and revealing all the insider's tax-avoidance tricks and tactics for you to use in your investing.

ARE YOU READY FOR 35,000 ON THE DOW?

Chances are, you'll need to use all the tax breaks available. Many observers expect the coming years will be great ones for investors. Harry S. Dent, a consultant and economic forecaster based in Moss Beach, California, forecasts the Dow Jones Industrial Average will hit 35,000 by 2008.

The Stock Market's Baby Boom

Dent's optimism stems from demographics. For the average individual, saving accelerates from age 35 to age 68 while spending peaks around age 46.5. Thus, both patterns are moving up between ages 35 and 46.5. Money moves into stocks at that stage of life, when families have both high discretionary income and a relatively long time before retirement.

As the century turns, the fabled baby boom generation is moving into that age cohort. The first boomers appeared in 1946, right after World War II, so they'll turn 55 in the year 2001, with their younger siblings right behind them. In 1987, there were about 20 million Americans in the 45 to 54 age bracket; that number is projected to crest at more than 40 million in 2008.

Impact: The baby boomers are moving into their peak spending and investing years, so the stock market is likely to bound from peak to peak.

History Lesson

If you participate in the stock market, such bullish views are welcome news. Dent is forecasting that the market will rise by about 16% per year.

Even if you take a less aggressive stance and assume, say, a 12% annual return (the average over the past 65 years) your money will double every six years.

THE MILLIONAIRE AT HOME

Think about that for awhile. Suppose you're 55, with a modest $200,000 invested in stocks.

✔ If you earn 12% for the next six years, your $200,000 will become $400,000.

✔ Assume another 12% return over the subsequent six years. Your money will double again, to $800,000. And that's just the money you have saved now.

✔ Assuming that you'll continue to save and invest over the intervening 12 years, you'll likely have over $1 million by then, perhaps well over $1 million.

By age 67, when you're ready to retire, you'll be a millionaire.

Tax Trap

Well, not really. Those numbers are all pretax. To make the most of the coming boom you need to minimize the tax bite on your income and on your wealth. If you understand these rules and implement some basic planning strategies—the strategies revealed in this book—you can turn these years of prosperity into a long-term wealth-building machine that literally can pay out millions to you and your loved ones.

HOW TO READ THIS BOOK

We've organized this book along fairly simple lines.

First, we explain the tax implications of the investments you're likely to hold: stocks, bonds, mutual funds, real estate.

Next, we cover tax-favored ways of saving for retirement through

IRAs, 401(k)s, and so on. (We also explain the tax angles involved in making the most of your Social Security benefits.)

From there we go on to cover life insurance and related vehicles. Life insurance enjoys some of the richest tax benefits in the tax code, a situation likely to persist.

We provide special coverage for business owners who decide their best investment is their own company.

Before winding up with some tax-wise final thoughts, we shift our focus from income tax savings to estate tax savings. After all, why devote your energies to cutting income tax, at rates no higher than 39.6% (under current federal law), if your family winds up paying estate tax at rates up to 55%?

Our goal is to help you slash all of your tax bills, leaving more of your wealth for yourself, your loved ones, and your favored causes.

Chapter

Getting Started with Stocks

Every year, investors pour billions of dollars into mutual funds, especially stock funds. And, every year, investors are shocked by the tax bills those funds generate.

When taxes are considered, the old-fashioned way is better: Buy individual stocks instead. As long as you buy and hold with minimal trading, your tax bill from your investments will be negligible.

THE MUTUAL FUND MINEFIELD

To understand the advantages of buying stocks directly, consider the tax rules governing mutual funds. Federal tax law requires that mutual funds distribute at least 98% of their *ordinary income* and net realized gains for a calendar year within that same calendar year.

Suppose, for example, ABC Growth Fund invested $1 million in Microsoft back in the 1980s. Since then it has held on to Microsoft, watching the stock appreciate—and generating no tax obligation.

In the year 2000, concerned about the company's battles with the government, ABC Growth Fund sells its Microsoft stake, which has grown to $20 million.

ordinary income
taxable income that receives no favorable tax treatment.

1

The company has a long-term gain of $19 million, practically all of which must be distributed to share-holders.

FUNDS CHURN, INVESTORS ARE BURNED

Of course, ABC Growth Fund won't have only one sale of its Microsoft stock during the year. More likely, it will have dozens of sales, each of which generates a gain or a loss. (The average stock fund has a *turnover rate* greater than 80%, so a typical mutual fund is a fairly active trader.)

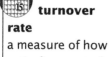 **turnover rate**
a measure of how actively a mutual fund trades its holdings. A fund with a 100% turnover rate holds each in-vestment for an average of one year before sell-ing it.

The net trading gains must be distributed annually. If ABC Growth Fund winds up the year with $50 million in net gains and there are 50 million shares outstanding, it will distribute $1 per share.

MANY UNHAPPY RETURNS

Such distributions are taxable to you, whether you rein-vest your capital gains distributions and thus collect no cash. That's true even if the fund loses value in a year.

This happens frequently. Indeed, in times of market trouble investors bail out of losing funds, and those in-vestors who stay behind (or buy in shortly before the dis-tribution date) get larger per-share distributions, so they owe more tax.

If you invest after the fund enjoyed big gains but be-fore the distribution, you'll still owe tax on the distribu-tion you receive.

In this example, ABC Growth Fund sells Microsoft and other long-term holdings as well, winding up distrib-uting $1 per share. Suppose you bought ABC Growth Fund at $20 per share just before the $1 per share distrib-ution (which drops the price to $19 per share). You would get $1 per share in distributions, on which you'll owe tax. In effect, you're paying a tax on a return of your own capital.

SHORT GAINS, LARGE PAIN

The Taxpayer Relief Act of 1997 provided a cut in the capital gains tax, and subsequent legislation in 1998 enhanced this tax break. Now, if you hold a stock, mutual fund share, or other investment for more than one year, any gain will be taxed no more than 20% (down from 28%), even if you are in a higher tax bracket.

On the other hand, when you buy mutual funds, net realized gains must be distributed to investors each year. Some distributions will be short-term capital gains, taxable at rates up to 39.6%; only if the fund has held the shares for more than 12 months will shareholders get the benefit of the 20% rate.

It makes no difference whether you reinvest the short-term capital gains distribution; it makes no difference how long you've held the shares of that mutual fund. If you own the fund in a taxable account, you'll owe short-term capital gains tax at rates up to 39.6%. (Any *dividends* passed through to investors also will be taxed at ordinary rates up to 39.6%.)

> **dividends** payments of profit by a corporation to its shareholders.

COSTLY COMBINATION

Most mutual funds are managed to maximize pretax rather than after-tax results, so mutual fund distributions tend to be a mix of short- and long-term gains. Although the end result will vary according to your tax bracket, your state tax situation, and your fund's trading practices, you can expect to pay around 25% of each annual distribution in tax.

Suppose, for example, Jane Jones has $10,000 invested in XYZ Value Fund. In 1999, XYZ posted a total return of 25%. Of her $2,500 return, though, about $1,000 (40%, the industry norm) came to her in the form of distributions. At an effective 25% tax rate, Jane had to pay $250, knocking her actual return from $2,500 (25%) down to $2,250 (22.5%).

Long-term, losing that much in taxes each year can make a huge difference in the wealth you accumulate.

ROLL YOUR OWN

For more control and lower tax, you can buy individual stocks. Trading through a discount broker, costs will be minor: Online trades may be under $10 apiece.

Then, you can just hold on to your stocks indefinitely. You'll owe tax on the dividends you receive, but the average dividend yield on the S&P 500 is around 1.5%. At a 30% tax rate, your tax bill would be a token 0.45%.

CASHING IN

Buy-and-hold is a fine investment strategy, but what if you need to get your hands on some cash? Do you have to sell shares and trigger a taxable gain?

✔ If your stocks appreciate and you want to cash in some of your profits, you can borrow up to 50% against the full value of your stocks. The interest you pay likely will be deductible, as an offset to taxable investment interest.

✔ Another possibility is to sell off your winners. You can specify which shares you want to sell, choosing those that will generate the smallest tax bill. And you can sell off some losers as an offset, reducing or eliminating your tax bill.

Impact: With some savvy planning you can wind up each year with a net realized loss of $3,000, fully deductible, while you let most of your winners ride.

MISSION: CONTROL

You can do some of the same things with mutual funds that you can do with individual stocks. You can match winners with losers; you can borrow against your funds if they're held in a brokerage account.

However, with individual stocks you're likely to have

more variability from one issue to another, which will provide you with increased flexibility for tax planning. And you'll certainly have more control—you'll realize taxable gains when you choose to do so, not at the whim of some fund manager.

BOLD NEW WORLD

As mentioned earlier, recent changes in tax law lowered the maximum tax on capital gains from 28% to 20% on assets held more than 12 months. These changes created many new opportunities for investors.

Stocks beat bonds—by a wider margin than ever. As an investment, equity is preferable to debt, provided you diversify your holdings and stay in for the long term. Now that the tax on any gains is reduced, stocks look even better.

Impact: Don't rush to switch from stocks to bonds as you near retirement. You're better off keeping your money invested in *equities* and then meeting any cash needs by selling stocks. Changes in the tax law decrease the tax you'll pay when liquidating appreciated securities.

> **equities**
> ownership interests. Publicly traded stocks are often called equities.

Borrowing to buy stocks or real estate makes more sense. The after-tax cost of borrowing remains the same, while your after-tax gains may be greater.

Suppose, for example, you take a $10,000 margin loan to buy stocks, paying 8% ($800) per year in interest. In a 39.6% tax bracket, deducting the interest on your income tax return will save you $317 in tax, so your net cost will be only $483 per year.

Suppose the stocks you buy go up 10% ($1,000) per year. Under prior law, your net annual gain would have been $720, after paying capital gains tax at 28%; now your after-tax gain is $800 a year.

Retirement plans are good—but not as great. Under current tax law you'll need a commitment to higher returns (perhaps by investing more in stocks) and longer holding periods for investments inside deductible individual retirement accounts (IRAs), 401(k)s, simplified employee pensions (SEPs), and other plans.

marginal tax rate
the rate at which your last dollar (or your next dollar) of income will be taxed. Also known as your tax bracket.

long-term capital gains
profit from the sale of an asset held more than a year. Under current law, the maximum tax rate is 20%.

Unfortunately, all money coming out of such retirement plans would be taxed at your top *marginal tax rate* (at present as high as 39.6%), no matter how that income was derived. In essence, you lose the capital gain tax break that exists inside the plan.

Nevertheless, the longer you'll defer taxes, the better a retirement plan will work. Such plans remain particularly effective if you'll have a holding period of 20 years or more.

Tax brackets count, too. If you think you'll be in a lower bracket when you withdraw your money, perhaps after you retire, tax-deferred plans still can be very big winners.

Diversification may come easier. Your portfolio may be overweighted in shares of your employer's stock, stock options, or shares of one company given to you by family members. Selling some of those shares will reduce your exposure to one stock but may generate sizable capital gains.

Now, rebalancing your portfolio becomes less expensive because you'll owe only 20% on *long-term capital gains*.

Big Break for Small Fry

Here's a vital break for parents of young children:

The tax law also provides a bargain 10% capital gains tax rate. Taxpayers in the 15% income tax bracket pay only 10% tax on capital gains. That includes single filers with less than $25,000 in taxable income (about $45,000, filing jointly).

So here's a winning strategy: If you're cashing in appreciated securities to pay college bills, give them to your children before selling.

As long as your kids are older than 13, they likely can sell the shares and pay tax at just 10%; then they can use the net proceeds for college. You and your spouse can give away $20,000 worth of assets per year, per recipient, with no gift tax consequences.

Elder Shelter

Another super strategy:

If you're helping to support elderly parents, give them appreciated securities instead of cash. Again, your parents may be able to sell and pay tax at a bargain 10% rate.

NOW FOR THE NEGATIVES

Unfortunately, there's a downside to lower rates on long-term capital gains: The *basis step-up* has come down in value.

At your death, shares you bequeath get a step-up in *basis* to current value. For example, suppose you have a portfolio of stocks you bought for $100,000, now worth $500,000. If you die tomorrow and your son inherits, his basis in those shares moves up to $500,000. He can sell them for $500,000 and owe no capital gains tax on the $400,000 profit.

The value of this tax break is smaller now (an $80,000 savings at a 20% rate) than it was under prior law (when the savings would have been $112,000 at a 28% rate).

Formerly, many investors were frozen in place: To get the basis step-up, they held on to appreciated assets until death. Now that this tax break has been devalued, you can take some gains, pay tax at 20%, and reinvest the net proceeds where opportunities seem greater.

Ironically, charitable giving also has been devalued. The same reasoning that applies to basis step-ups also applies to using appreciated assets for charitable gifts. Under the new law, such gifts save 20 cents on the dollar, not 28 cents.

Charitable giving now depends even more on your philanthropic objectives and not as much on tax savings.

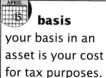

basis step-up
a tax break enjoyed by heirs to appreciated property. When you inherit an asset your basis is increased to its value at the owner's death, effectively eliminating the tax on all the gains that were not cashed in.

basis
your basis in an asset is your cost for tax purposes.

DOWNPLAY DIVIDENDS

With all this emphasis on capital gains, what about dividends? Isn't it marvelous to invest in AT&T or Con Edison and receive a check every three months?

Not always. From a taxpayer's point of view, buying dividend-paying stocks is unattractive.

✔ Dividends are near historic lows, with the average stock in the Standard & Poor's 500 paying around 1.5%, as of this writing.

✔ The dividend income you receive will be taxed as ordinary income, with rates up to 39.6%. If you owe state or even local income tax, you could lose 40% to 45% of your dividends in taxes.

✔ That tax is due every year, even if you reinvest your dividends.

✔ On the other hand, when a stock you hold appreciates, no tax is due as long as you don't sell.

✔ Even when you sell a stock at a profit, federal income tax is capped at 20%, as long as you have held the stock more than 12 months.

BEYOND THE BORDERS

global funds
investment pools that can invest anywhere in the world, including the United States.

country funds
investment pools that invest in one particular foreign country.

Financial planners and investment advisers routinely recommend some commitment to foreign stocks as part of a diversified portfolio. Thus, some American investors have moved into foreign stocks and stock funds, such as *global funds* or *country funds*.

You don't really need foreign stocks, but history shows that there are advantages to diversification. As of this writing, the U.S. market is strong while foreign stocks have been down, but that may not be the case in the future.

As recently as 1990, the U.S. economy seemed to be flat on its back while the Japanese seemed to dominate the world and the Japanese stock market had enjoyed a long boom. Since then, the U.S. stock market has soared while the Japanese market has fallen from 38,000 to 18,000.

UPS AND DOWNS

The Japanese market's 1990s slump of more than 50% can be compared to the U.S. experience in 1929 to 1932, when our market fell by 68%. Since then there has not been a decline of that magnitude, but the 1964 to 1981 period saw U.S. stocks stagnate.

Throughout that time frame, the annual return on the S&P 500 remained below 7% per year, which failed to keep up with inflation. If American stocks hit another such slow-down in the future, investors may be glad to have some money in other, possibly faster-growing markets.

Indeed, the question is not *whether* you'll invest in foreign economies but *how* you'll invest. If you invest in Coca-Cola or Boeing or almost any major American cor-poration, you have a stake in foreign business because these companies sell outside the United States. You need to decide if you're content to have that sort of a foreign stake or if you're going to invest some money directly in foreign securities.

EXPANDING THE ENVELOPE: ADRs

To some professionals, the advantage of placing some money outside the United States is not diversification. They look at foreign economies as being more options to consider when you're looking for the best investments. Just as you might be excited by the profit prospects of a certain company, so you may be optimistic about the growth potential of a given country or region of the world. If you invest only in the United States you limit yourself and stand to miss out on some great companies.

Many foreign companies trade in the United States as *American Depositary Receipts (ADRs)*, which resemble common stocks. You can pick your own stocks, selecting among the largest foreign companies, through ADRs. If you select well, you can hold on to your ADRs and enjoy untaxed appreciation until you decide to sell, at favorable long-term capital gains rates.

Bank Notes

How is it possible for U.S. investors to invest in individ-ual foreign companies? U.S. banks hold foreign shares in

American Depositary Receipts (ADRs) investments that take the place of shares in foreign companies. ADRs trade in the United States on virtually the same terms as the shares of U.S. stocks.

custody and issue ADRs, each of which represents one share (or a specified number of shares) of the underlying foreign stock. Citibank, J. P. Morgan, and the Bank of New York are the leading issuers of ADRs.

Over 1,700 foreign stocks from dozens of countries trade as ADRs, with more joining the list all the time. Estimates put the total capitalization of the ADR market at more than $500 billion.

After they're issued, ADRs trade just like U.S. stocks, on the leading exchanges or over the counter. All transactions are handled in U.S. dollars. You collect dividends, if they're paid, and you can sell whenever you wish.

In essence, with ADRs you can control your investments while you avoid the hassles of trading foreign stocks.

POSSIBLE PITFALLS

Nevertheless, ADR investors won't avoid all the perils of investing in foreign stocks. You don't have to exchange currency to purchase ADRs, but their prices are still influenced by fluctuating currency values. The pricing of ADRs reflects the U.S. dollar value of a foreign security, so currency movements will work to your advantage when the currency of the country you're investing in drops in relation to the dollar.

However, the opposite is also true: When foreign currencies strengthen in relation to the U.S. dollar, the value of ADRs drops. For example, if you buy a Japanese company that appreciates 10% in yen but the U.S. dollar declines 5% versus the yen, your gain would actually be 5%: the 10% stock price gain minus the 5% currency loss.

Therefore, you might see a situation in which Telefonos de Mexico, the Mexican phone company, has a flat day in Mexico while the company's ADR rises or declines in the United States by 5% or 10% the same day because of currency movement. Such fluctuations may be reversed the next day, if currency trading goes the other way. Overall, ADRs tend to track the performance of their corresponding foreign securities.

Moreover, some ADRs often are thinly traded, compared with the company's shares in its home market. As a result, it may not be easy to sell them quickly. However, brokers who specialize in trading ADRs can always instruct the custodian to sell the underlying securities as a way of liquidating ADRs.

Countless Tax Collectors

Taxes are another issue that all investors in foreign stocks, including holders of ADRs, have to contend with. The dividends you receive are in U.S. dollars but the payments represent foreign dividends on the underlying stocks.

These dividends, paid in foreign currencies to the custodian bank, are then converted to U.S. currency for payment to ADR investors. Therefore, U.S. investors owe foreign taxes on these dividends.

Suppose, for example, you own 100 shares of an ADR and the company declares a dividend of 50 cents per share. Instead of a $50 dividend, you might receive $42.50 (if 15% is withheld) or even $35.

Paper Chase

In these circumstances, you have a choice. You can deduct the withheld taxes on Schedule A as an itemized deduction or you can file Form 1116 to claim a foreign tax credit. Generally, a credit is more valuable than a deduction, but the effort involved in wrestling with Form 1116 may not be worth the tax savings.

Tax Tip Until the 1998 tax year, the only way to get this foreign tax credit was to file Form 1116—a complicated, time-consuming process. Now, though, most couples with credits of $600 or less can take them directly on their Form 1040, the basic tax return. For single filers, you can avoid Form 1116 if you had no more than $300 worth of foreign tax withheld.

Impact: If you invest in ADRs through a tax-deferred retirement plan, you can't use either the deduction or the credit. In effect, the foreign tax withheld is an outright loss. Thus, you might want to hold any ADRs in a taxable account rather than inside a retirement plan.

EASING YOUR WAY INTO ADRs

Several banks now offer dividend reinvestment plans for ADRs. For example, J. P. Morgan has a shareholder services program (800-749-1687) that includes more than 60 companies, from AMN AMRO of the Netherlands to Zeneca Group of the United Kingdom. If you become a shareholder in one or more of these companies you'll receive all of your companies' news releases, annual reports, proxy materials, and so on without any delays.

The J. P. Morgan program permits investors to purchase shares regularly—weekly, monthly, quarterly, or annually—and thus reap the advantages of dollar-cost averaging. Money for such purchases can be withdrawn automatically from your checking account while dividends can be reinvested regularly as well.

Investors in this program get quarterly statements summarizing all of their ADR activity. In this program, ADRs are held electronically so there are no certificates to store; when it comes time to sell, investors can do so with a toll-free phone call.

Ground Rules

With the J. P. Morgan program, initial purchases must be at least $250; additional purchases may be as low as $50. Investors must pay a $15 enrollment fee for each company they want to buy. Dividend reinvestments are subject to a 5% fee, up to a $2.50 cap, while direct purchases or sales are charged $5 per transaction, plus 12 cents per share (an additional $12 for a round lot of 100 shares).

With this fee structure it probably won't pay to invest only $50 at a time because the $5 fee amounts to a steep 10% of your $50. However, the fee represents a much lower charge if you invest, say, $500 per transaction. Investing $500 in Barclays Bank, for example, while the ADR trades at $90, would generate a fee of around $5.65 ($5 plus 12 cents each for approximately five and a half shares), slightly more than 1% of the total.

To help investors keep up with ADRs, J. P. Morgan operates a web site (www.adr.com) that contains information on about 400 of the most widely held and actively traded ADRs. The site features a live ticker with current stock quotes, trading volumes, and news updates. Thus, you can stay home and literally have the world of investing at your fingertips.

MARGINAL METHODS

If you think the stock market surge of the 1980s and 1990s will continue, you can increase your profit potential by buying stocks or stock funds on *margin*. Using margin to invest will raise your returns if stocks go up but you'll also lose more if stocks fall. Indeed, during the October 1987 stock market crash many margin investors took painful losses.

To decide whether to invest on margin, you should know the basics. Margin investors use borrowed money—money that's borrowed from a broker rather than from a banker. Interest rates are pegged to the broker's call rate, which is listed in the daily newspapers.

Most brokers charge anywhere from 0.5% to 2% above the broker's call rate; if that rate is 8%, margin loans would be in the 8.5% to 10% range, with the lowest rates reserved for margin loans over $50,000. Interest, which is payable monthly, is usually subtracted from the equity in your margin account.

TWO FOR THE MONEY

There are, in essence, two ways to buy stocks or stock funds on margin. One way is to *leverage* borrowed money to make the initial purchase. Investing in this manner can

margin
the amount an investor deposits with a broker when borrowing money from that broker. Margin can be in the form of cash or securities.

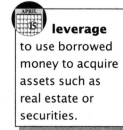

leverage
to use borrowed money to acquire assets such as real estate or securities.

help you get more participation in equities if you're low on cash. For example, if you have only $5,000 to invest you can buy $10,000 worth of stocks, with a margin account.

The other way to buy stocks on margin is to borrow against securities you already hold in your brokerage account. Only securities held in *street name* can be used. This excludes securities you hold personally, in your own name.

 street name
the practice of having securities held by your broker rather than keeping the certificates yourself.

THE 50% SOLUTION

Whichever approach you use, margin loans are backed by securities held in your brokerage account. For most securities, the maximum initial margin allowed is 50%: You can borrow $50,000 on margin if you have $100,000 worth of stocks, bonds, and mutual funds. For Treasury bonds held by your broker, the maximum initial margin is 90%.

Although the Federal Reserve and the New York Stock Exchange set the basic regulations, each brokerage firm has its own rules on margin. Some brokers don't allow margin on securities they consider too speculative, such as stocks selling for less than $5 per share. Moreover, you can't use margin in tax-deferred retirement accounts such as IRAs and profit-sharing plans.

LEARNING TO LOVE LEVERAGE

To see how margin can help increase your potential profits, assume you have $100,000 invested in stocks that can be used for margin. If so, maximum margin could boost your holdings to $150,000 worth of stocks.

If those stocks go up by 20% in the next 12 months, you'd have a $30,000 gain, not a $20,000 gain on a $100,000 portfolio. Even if you paid 9% interest ($4,500 on a $50,000 loan), you'd have a $25,500 net gain. Using margin would have boosted your return by $5,500.

CULTIVATING THE TAX CODE

After-tax, the results may be even better.

- ✔ Interest on margin loans can be deducted against taxable investment income.
- ✔ If you're able to deduct your margin loan interest, your real cost of money may be only around 5%.
- ✔ In the meanwhile, any appreciation on the stocks you hold will build up untaxed until gains are realized, and even then those gains may be favorably taxed as long-term capital gains.

The best of all possible worlds, then, would be for you to borrow at 5%, after-tax, to earn 15% or 20%, tax-deferred.

DEPENDABLE DEDUCTIONS

Thus, when you take margin loans for successful stock market investments, you may be using deductible dollars to buy assets where the unrealized appreciation is tax-deferred and likely to be taxed later at favorable rates. The trick is to make sure your margin loans are fully deductible.

How can you do that?

- ✔ Use margin loans solely to buy securities. If you use the loan proceeds to buy a car or pay college tuition the interest won't be deductible.
- ✔ Make sure you have enough *investment income* to offset fully the margin loan interest you pay. Investment income includes interest and dividends but you can elect to include capital gains, too, if necessary.

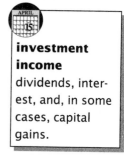

investment income
dividends, interest, and, in some cases, capital gains.

What if you have to pay $10,000 in margin loan interest and receive only $7,000 in investment income this year? The extra $3,000 can be carried forward and deducted against investment income in the future.

MARGIN AND MUNICIPAL BONDS DON'T MIX

If you're a margin investor, you also might want to move from tax-exempt bonds to Treasuries because margin interest isn't deductible if it's used to "purchase or carry" municipal bonds or muni bond funds. Suppose, for example, municipal bonds represent 10% of the assets in your brokerage account. If you incur $10,000 worth of margin interest you can write off no more than $9,000.

Even if you keep your munis in a separate account, the Internal Revenue Service (IRS) might contend that the loans helped you carry the bonds. You're required to report tax-exempt interest income on page 1 of your tax return, which makes it easy for the IRS to match up this income with deductions for investment interest that you paid.

STOCKS FALL, BROKERS CALL

Therefore, tax benefits can amplify the benefits of investing on margin—if your stocks go up. Unfortunately, your stocks are not guaranteed to gain 15% or 20%, or any amount at all. When stocks fall, losses are magnified by margin loans, and when stocks fall sharply, investors using margin have to face the prospect of *margin calls.*

margin call
a demand from a broker to add more cash or securities to your margin deposit.

Suppose you borrow $50,000 against your $100,000 portfolio and your stocks fall by 10%, so they're worth $90,000. Your broker likely won't worry much, with $90,000 worth of assets securing a $50,000 loan.

However, if your stocks keep sinking and their value dips to $70,000, your broker will start to be concerned. (Many brokers have an informal rule that a 28% drop on 50% margin accounts will generate a margin call.) When you get a "house call," your broker will ask you to reduce the outstanding loan balance by putting in some cash or to increase the collateral by putting more securities into your margin account.

What if you don't comply? Your broker can sell your securities and use the proceeds for loan repayment. Usually you'll have a week to meet a market call but that may not be the case in volatile markets. In the 1987 crash many margin investors had their stocks called away before they had a chance to cover.

PROCEED WITH CAUTION

Using maximum (50%) margin may expose you to margin calls because a 28% drop in the price of a stock is not that unusual. If you'd like to be on safer ground, yet still have a chance for extra returns, you can use less margin.

✔ Borrow 33% and you won't get a margin call until your account value falls by 50%, which is less likely to happen.

✔ At 20% margin, you're not apt to get a call until there's a 70% loss of value—and it's likely you will have bailed out of the stock before that point.

Therefore, if you have a $100,000 portfolio and you borrow to bring it up to $120,000, say, or $133,000, you'll have more market participation without much risk of having to dip into other assets to meet margin calls. You need to monitor your stocks carefully when you buy on margin. Set your lower limits in advance and sell at a loss if your stocks fall to that level.

Impact: Using low margin levels may enable you to keep your loan in place indefinitely. You'd have a long-term loan outstanding at a reasonable rate, after-tax, while you plow the money into stocks, where the long-term returns are likely to exceed your cost of debt service.

RISKY BUSINESS

What are the risks of this strategy? Using margin is still using margin, whether it's 20% or 50%. If your stocks go down, your losses will be magnified. You need a strong stomach to use margin to invest in stocks.

Long-term investors with well-balanced stock portfolios are likely to post superior returns over most time periods. Using margin will enhance any gains because you'll have more stock in play. As long as you can ride out the downs, you'll be in a position to cash in on the ups. If you use margin in moderation rather than to the max, you may well have a smoother path to higher stock market profits.

Chapter

(Stock) Options Plays

I f you work for a publicly held company, chances are a portion of your compensation comes in the form of *stock options*. Since they're part of your income, stock options are subject to income tax and are therefore a fertile area for tax planning.

Stock options may be incentive stock options (ISOs) or nonqualified stock options (NQSOs). The former are a better deal because:

✔ Neither the grant nor the exercise of an ISO is a taxable event.

✔ With an ISO, taxes are due only when the underlying stock is sold, and capital gains rates apply.

> **stock options**
> the rights to acquire common stock at a given price during a preset time period.

KEEP YOUR EYE ON THE CALENDAR

In order to get the benefit of capital gains rates, you can't sell the underlying stock until two years have passed since the option grant and one year since the option exercise.

Suppose, for example, that Bob Jones was granted an ISO to buy 1,000 shares of ABC Co. on February 1, 1999. On February 1, 2000, he exercises his option. To get capital gains treatment (a 20% rate) he must wait until after February 1, 2001, to sell the shares.

PATIENCE MAY BE PRUDENT

Whenever you exercise an ISO, the spread between the grant price and the exercise price is an adjustment for the alternative minimum tax (AMT), so you need to exercise ISOs with caution. (See Chapter 16 for more on the AMT.)

Despite the tax advantages, if ISOs fall sharply after exercise, your tax break becomes a burden. Suppose you exercise an ISO at $5 per share when your company's stock is at $100. Even if the stock retreats, you'll still owe capital gains tax (20%) on the spread ($95), for a tax obligation of $19 per share.

 Tax Tip You can make a "disqualifying disposition" by selling the shares in the year of exercise, if that works out to be less taxing. You'll owe ordinary income tax, but on a smaller gain. The earlier in the year you exercise an ISO, the more flexibility you'll have.

COMMON SENSE

If your stock options are not ISOs then they're NQSOs. The latter are more common. For employers, ISOs typically are not deductible. Therefore, most companies issue NQSOs, which provide a deduction at the time they're exercised.

Individuals pay tax on NQSOs when they're exercised. For example, suppose Mary Smith is granted NQSOs to buy shares of XYZ Co. at $10 per share. When she exercises her options, XYZ trades at $16 per share so Mary reports income of $6 per share.

As a result, Mary's basis in her new XYZ shares is $16 per share. Any subsequent sale will be eligible for long-term capital gains treatment, provided she meets the holding period rules, starting from her date of exercise.

SOONER OR LATER

With either type of stock option, deciding when to exercise is a concern. The longer you wait (until the option's expiration date), the more leverage you have because you're participating in the stock's market moves with no cash outlay.

Waiting until just before expiration increases your risk of a break in the stock price. Therefore, you might prefer a staged exercise. You could sell some of the acquired shares, pay tax, and reinvest in other stocks to diversify your portfolio.

> **Tax Tip** Phasing in ISO exercises works particularly well if your annual income stays below $150,000 ($112,500 for single filers). Above those levels you begin to lose an AMT exemption.

If you wait until year-end you'll get an idea of your income so you'll know how many NQSOs you can exercise without moving into a higher tax bracket.

Suppose your income this year will be in the 31% bracket. You might exercise enough options (and add enough income) to use up that tax bracket in full but not spill over into the 36% bracket.

✔ If you're planning to move to a low-tax state, wait until moving to exercise NQSOs.

✔ If you expect to be in a lower tax bracket after retirement, wait until then to exercise NQSOs, provided that such leeway is permitted by your employer. You may be required to exercise or forfeit all your options within 90 days after leaving the company. Even with a short time window, you might be able to defer exercise until the following year, when you'll be in a lower bracket.

GIVEAWAY GAME

If you're concerned about future estate taxes, lifetime gifts of stock options may trim your taxable estate.

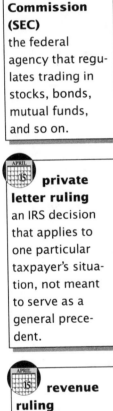

Incentive stock options (ISOs) are not transferable except in case of death; even transfers to your spouse are forbidden. However, a 1996 ruling by the *Securities and Exchange Commission (SEC)* paved the way for giving NQSOs to relatives or to trusts established for their benefit. In order for you to make such gifts, your employer's stock option plan must authorize transfers.

In addition, the IRS has issued a *private letter ruling* that giving away NQSOs does not trigger income and payroll tax. Those taxes won't be due until the recipient exercises the options.

When the options are exercised, the executive who earned them will owe the income tax. In essence, you're making a larger gift to the recipient but no gift tax is owed on the income tax payment.

APRIL 15 Securities and Exchange Commission (SEC) the federal agency that regulates trading in stocks, bonds, mutual funds, and so on.

APRIL 15 private letter ruling an IRS decision that applies to one particular taxpayer's situation, not meant to serve as a general precedent.

APRIL 15 revenue ruling an IRS announcement that is meant to indicate the agency's official stance on a tax issue.

A DISCOURAGING WORD

Through 1997 and early 1998, many executives gave away newly granted but unvested stock options to family members. Such options could be assigned low values for gift tax purposes and all the appreciation would be out of the executive's taxable estate.

In April 1998, though, the IRS issued a *revenue ruling* to stop this maneuver. The IRS position is that options can't be given away until they're vested.

Not everybody agrees with the IRS, so a future court case may result in a reversal. For now, though, giving away unvested stock options puts you on a collision course with the IRS.

At the same time, giving away vested options is approved by the IRS. If you own vested options that have low current values but great future potential, they may make ideal gifts.

VALUABLE LESSONS

How do you put a value on options that you give away? The IRS wants you to use the Black-Scholes option pricing model or something similar, without any discounts.

For a rough idea of an option's valuation, add one-third to the stock price and deduct the exercise price.

Suppose you hold stock options with a $22 exercise price while the stock sells at $30. The gift tax value likely will be around $18: $30 + $10 − $22 = $18.

Before making such gifts, you should hire a reputable appraiser to provide a valuation, which might be lower than the one the IRS would prefer. If your valuation is challenged, you'll do no worse than the IRS's number, so why start there?

REVEAL, DON'T CONCEAL

In addition, make certain you fully disclose any discounts you claim on a gift tax return. The IRS has three years to audit your return. If there's no question raised in this period, the statute of limitations will prevent any future dispute.

Besides estate-reduction gifts to younger family members, consider giving stock options to your spouse. This can equalize estates and allow full use of the gift/estate unified tax credit, no matter which spouse dies first.

OPTION PLAYS II

Don't confuse the employer stock options just described with listed stock options. Such listed options trade like stocks; options on hundreds of different stocks are available.

To truly make the most of these vehicles you need to know the tax implications. There are two main varieties of options: calls and puts.

Calls

strike price
the price at which an option can be exercised.

These are options to buy a security or a derivative instrument at a certain *strike price* within a certain time period.

A Cisco/January/65 call, for example, is an option to buy Cisco Systems at $65 per share between the date of purchase and a specified date in January.

Listed options cover 100 shares. Thus, if this option is priced at 10 in the newspaper listing, investors would pay $1,000 for an option to buy 100 shares of Cisco.

Puts

These are options to sell at a certain price, up to a certain date.

A Cisco/January/75 put is an option to sell Cisco at $75 per share between the date of purchase and a date in January. If the listing reads 6, investors would pay $600 for an option to sell 100 shares of Cisco.

FUNDAMENTAL FOURSOME

There are four fundamental transactions you can make with listed options on individual stocks: buy a call, buy a put, sell a call, or sell a put.

BIG BANG FOR YOUR BUCKS: BUY A CALL

Buying a call allows you to participate in a market move at a relatively low price because an option costs less than the underlying stock.

If the stock goes up, you'll enjoy a greater percentage gain. However, you can lose all of the money you've paid for the call if the stock does not perform well.

To see the profit potential of listed options, consider what happened on May 13, 1999. A series of favorable economic reports and takeover news lifted bank stocks. J. P. Morgan rose $7.625 per share, to $146.75, a gain of 5.5% in a single day.

The same day, though, other investors in J. P. Morgan gained 183%! They had invested in the May 140 call, which shot up from $3 to $8.50 eight days before its expiration date.

Before the news broke, J. P. Morgan was trading at $139.125. In the lingo of the options market the 140 call was *out of the money*, or worthless. Who would exercise an option to buy shares at $140 when those shares could be acquired for $139.125 on the open market?

However, when the stock shot up to $146.75, the option suddenly became *in the money*, or valuable. Holders of the option could acquire shares worth $146.75 by paying $140. This last-minute surge, from worthless to valuable, powered the option price from $3 to $8.50 and put enormous profits in the pockets of savvy option traders.

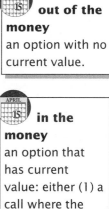

out of the money
an option with no current value.

in the money
an option that has current value: either (1) a call where the exercise price is below the trading price or (2) a put where the exercise price is above the trading price.

Tax Treatment

Buying a call on an individual stock is similar to buying the stock when it comes to taxes. You'll have a capital gain or loss, long- or short-term, depending on the holding period.

If you exercise a call and buy the underlying stock, all of your costs, including the option premium, are included in your cost basis in the stock. However, your holding period in the stock won't start until after you exercise the option.

COVER YOUR ANATOMY: BUY A PUT

What other option plays should you consider?

Buy a put. Buying a put locks in a selling price for a stock. Many investors buy puts on stocks they own. In this manner, investors with appreciated positions can protect their gains without triggering a capital gains tax, under current law.

Suppose you bought Cisco many years ago and have enjoyed substantial appreciation. Now, with the stock selling for more than $70 per share, you are uneasy about future prospects. You buy an October/65 put, which locks in a selling price if the stock skids.

> **Tax Tip** Simply buying the put does not trigger a long-time capital gain, under the tax law in effect as of this writing.

If you buy a $65 put and your stock falls below $65 you can sell your shares for $65. In this case, you might recognize a long-term capital gain, which would be reduced by the amount you paid for the put.

If the stock rises or just holds its own, your put may expire without being exercised. Why would you sell Cisco for $65 if it's trading for, say, $70? You'd have a capital loss from your put purchase that can be used to offset taxable gains, although the use of that loss may have to be deferred.

covered option
the obligation to sell a security you already own, on certain terms.

naked option
the obligation to sell a security you don't own. If you have to sell it you'll have to buy it first, at any price, so your potential loss is enormous.

SELL-SIDE STRATEGY: SELL A CALL

You can trade options by selling as well as buying them.

You can sell an option on shares you own (*covered option*) or on shares you don't own (*naked option*), which means you're speculating the stock price will fall. Some investors regularly sell covered calls to squeeze income from the stock market, at the expense of potential capital gains.

Stiff-Arming the Taxman

The cash you receive when selling a call is not considered taxable income when received. Instead, tax consequences aren't triggered until the option expires, is sold, or is exercised, which may be in the next taxable year. Thus, selling a call can provide tax deferral.

If the underlying stock stagnates or drops, the call option you sold may expire worthless. You'd have a short-term capital gain equal to the amount of the premium you received. If you wish, you can sell another call and receive another premium.

If the stock price exceeds the exercise price of a call you've sold, the underlying stock probably will be called away. You'll have a short-term or long-term capital gain on the disposition of the stock, with the option premium added to your selling price for tax purposes.

> **Tax Tip** If you sell a covered call and the underlying stock rises above the strike price, you can avoid an exercise (and the resulting tax obligation, if the stock has appreciated since you purchased it) by buying back the call. You'll lose money on the options trade; that capital loss may have to be deferred under the tax rules.

GOING FOR THE CYCLE: SELL A PUT

What's the fourth basic strategy with listed options?

Sell a put. Again, you'll receive cash from the option sale. In essence, you're promising to buy a stock in the future, so you're hoping that (1) the stock will go up in price and the put will not be exercised, or (2) the stock price will go down so you will be able to buy the stock tomorrow at a lower price.

Suppose you sell a Cisco/October/70 put. If the stock moves up to $75 the put won't be exercised and you'll keep the option premium. You'll recognize a short-term capital gain when the option expires.

If the stock goes down and the option is exercised you'll wind up buying the stock. The put premium you received will reduce your basis in the shares.

BROADER EXPOSURE

These four transactions apply to options on a single stock. You also can buy options on broad-based market indexes (such as the Dow Jones Industrial Average or the Value Line Composite) and options on stock index futures (including the Standard & Poor's 500 and the New York Stock Exchange Composite).

Such options are subject to different tax rules:

✔ *Mark-to-market rule*. All such positions are treated as if sold at year-end, at the current price, and repurchased at the beginning of the next year.

✔ *60/40 rule*. The net gain or loss for the year is treated as 60% long-term and 40% short-term, regardless of the holding period. That includes phantom gains or losses reported under the mark-to-market rule as well as actual realized gains or losses.

Impact: For short-term traders these rules may be advantageous because gains (if any) on these options will be largely taxed at favorable long-term capital gains rates.

BITS OF BUNDLES

APRIL 15 **unit investment trusts (UITs)** an investment vehicle that pools money from many investors and buys a fixed portfolio of stocks and bonds. Investors' shares are called units.

As an alternative to stocks, consider investing through equity *unit investment trusts (UITs)*. Equity UITs may be the most cost-effective vehicles for individuals who want to own stocks in a particular sector. What's more, they help take the emotion out of investing.

✔ In the UIT format, securities are bundled together and sold in pieces to investors.

✔ Most brokers sell equity UITs, generally with a $1,000 minimum.

✔ UITs are unmanaged pools, meaning that the securities are unchanged throughout the life of the trust, except for unusual circumstances.

GOING TO THE DOGS

In the late 1970s and early 1980s, a time of high interest rates, fixed-income UITs were popular because they enabled investors to lock in those lofty yields. Now, most UITs are equity UITs.

With an equity UIT, a group of stocks is selected for a buy-and-hold strategy, so investors are buying an unmanaged collection of equities. So far, four types of equity UITs have emerged that fit into this format.

1. *Equity UITs that apply a set of rules.* Indeed, equity UITs first gained wide appeal as a way to participate in the "Dogs of the Dow" strategy.

This strategy (also known as "Dogs 10") calls for buying the 10 highest-yielding stocks among the 30 stocks that comprise the Dow Jones Industrial Average at the beginning of each year. A year later, replacements are made, if other stocks have moved into the top 10. (When a stock has a high yield, its dividend is a relatively large portion of its trading price; hence, high-yield stocks tend to be low-priced "dogs.") Long-term, an investor following this strategy would have reaped significant rewards.

Investors interested in a Dogs strategy likely would find it awkward to buy shares in the 10 companies and rearrange their portfolios each year. Thus, unit trusts provide a convenient way for investors to bet on the Dogs. (Another strategy said to produce even better results—the "Dogs 5," consisting of the lowest-priced stocks among the 10 Dogs—also can be replicated via unit trusts.)

The Dogs haven't been running well lately: This contrarian, value-oriented strategy wasn't in favor during the late 1990s. Meanwhile, other strategy-based UITs have emerged recently.

For example, some UITs offer a buyback portfolio consisting of financially sound companies that have reduced their shares outstanding through stock repurchases. Other equity UITs screen for stocks that have low price-to-sales ratios as well as share price momentum, a strategy supported by historical results.

2. *Index funds.* The Nasdaq 100, for example, includes the stocks that led the market in the late 1990s: Microsoft, Intel, Cisco Systems, Dell Computer. This portfolio was up 85% in 1998. Equity UITs provide a handy way to purchase this group of stocks.

3. *Sector funds.* Such equity UITs allow investors to get a fixed basket of stocks involved in, for example, the Internet or even e-commerce. Typically, sector UITs include 25 or 30 stocks, so investors have a broader exposure to the sector than they could get on their own.

4. *Geographic funds.* Some UITs specialize in companies headquartered in a particular state or in a region, such as the Pacific Coast.

BUY AND HOLD

No matter which type of equity UIT is chosen, the stocks are generally held for the term of the trust, typically from one to six years.

stock merger
a transaction in which the shareholders in the target company receive shares of stock in the acquiring company.

✔ If one of the stocks is acquired in a *stock merger*, the trust will just hold the new stock.

✔ If it's a *cash merger*, the cash will be distributed pro rata.

✔ Index UITs will change holdings when the index changes, which might mean a slight adjustment each year.

When the trust matures, investors can cash in or they can roll over the UIT by investing in a new trust. Indeed, the idea behind some strategy-based UITs is to keep renewing, year after year.

cash merger
a transaction in which one company acquires another by offering money to shareholders.

THE WAITING GAME

Whether they cash in or roll over UITs, investors will incur tax consequences.

✔ If the trust has increased in value, there will be a capital gain; such gains will be long-term because the trusts are virtually all designed to last more than one year.

✔ Dividends are taxable, too, whether the cash is distributed or reinvested in additional units.

Investors who want to defer the taxes have another option. When the trust matures they can request distributions "in-kind," meaning that they'll receive shares of each stock in the portfolio.

This will defer the tax consequences until the shares are sold. In some cases, this distribution option is limited to investments over a certain amount, perhaps $10,000.

EXIT STRATEGIES

Although equity UITs have maturities that stretch out up to six years, they are not *illiquid* investments. Values are set daily and there is a *secondary market*.

The firms selling the units may try to match buyers and sellers, and there are firms that act as market makers. In addition, the sponsors may provide liquidity.

ON THE PLUS SIDE

The equity UIT format offers advantages, according to proponents.

✔ Many investors run into trouble in the stock market because of emotion; following a certain strategy increases the predictability of results, and UITs are the only way to be sure that some strategies are really implemented. In essence, equity UITs may supply the discipline that investors need.

✔ The fact that equity UITs are unmanaged may be another advantage because you don't have to worry about turnover of portfolio managers. When that happens with

illiquid
not easily sold at a market price.

secondary market
a formal or informal network where securities that already have been issued may be bought and sold.

a mutual fund, investors are faced with tough decisions, but unit trusts don't have that problem.

✔ Perhaps most important, equity UITs can give you control over your portfolio.

When you buy a mutual fund, current holdings aren't disclosed. Data from the services that track mutual funds are old by the time they appear. Then, after you buy a fund you have no idea what the manager will do. With equity UITs you know exactly which companies you own, how many shares of each stock, and what they're worth.

Mutual funds, moreover, bear redemption risk—managers might have to sell into a falling market to meet redemptions. Conversely, they might have a great deal of new money to invest when the market is strong. UITs don't face this buy-high, sell-low pressure.

No Trades, No Taxable Gains, No Management Fees

In addition, UITs may be tax-efficient because no trading gains are passed through to investors each year. There are no management fees, so expenses may be lower than they are with an average equity mutual fund.

NO FREE LUNCH

commissions
compensation
paid to a broker
or other interme-
diary for arrang-
ing a securities
trade.

Annual expenses might be low but equity UITs certainly come with costs to investors. A typical equity UIT has a 2.75% front load; after that, the initial load is 1.75% on a rollover or a switch to another trust. In wrap programs (see Chapter 4), upfront sales *commissions* can be sharply reduced or even waived. Then you'll pay your adviser, as per your contractual agreement.

Altogether, equity UITs can be well worth the costs, as long as you pick the right sector and stick to your selection.

Chapter

3

Finding the Best Bond Bargains

When the world was plunged into fears of financial chaos in the summer of 1998, stocks slumped but U.S. Treasury bonds stood out. Indeed, Treasury bonds have proved to be the investment of choice for investors around the world in times of crisis. Does this mean that you should buy Treasuries for the fixed-income sector of your portfolio, banking on Treasuries to offset any future weakness in stocks?

That depends on your objectives. If you're primarily holding bonds to provide you with price appreciation during a global panic, then Treasuries are for you. What's more, Treasuries offer tax advantages.

BASIC TRAINING

Before deciding on whether to invest in Treasuries, you should know the basics:

✔ U.S. Treasury obligations represent debt of the U.S. government. They are considered safe investments because the government backs them with its "full faith and credit."

✔ U.S. Treasury obligations are also tax advantaged. Interest earned is exempt from both state and local income taxes.

✔ Treasuries include bills (short-term), notes (intermediate-term), bonds (long-term), and Series EE savings bonds.

✔ Treasury bills (or T-bills) typically mature in three months, six months, or one year. T-bills are sold at auction at a discount from face value (and later redeemed, at *maturity*, at face value) so no annual interest is paid. Therefore, the taxable interest income can be deferred until time of redemption.

✔ Treasury notes (T-notes) mature in 2 to 10 years. The interest rate, which is fixed, is paid semiannually.

✔ Treasury bonds (T-bonds) mature in 10 to 30 years. Like T-notes, the bonds' interest rate is fixed, and paid semiannually. Unlike T-notes, bonds may be callable.

maturity
the date when the issuer of a bond will repay bondholders a promised amount.

INFLATION-PROOF BONDS

Some Treasuries also may be appropriate if you want a hedge against inflation. Inflation-indexed Treasuries are available in various maturities.

yield
the periodic cash return on an investment: interest on a bond or a dividend on a stock.

If an inflation-indexed Treasury is priced to have a *yield* of 4.6%, for example, while a regular Treasury of the same maturity is priced to yield 5.8%, this implies a market forecast for inflation of 1.2%. If you think inflation will be higher, the inflation-indexed Treasury will be a better buy.

In 1999, 10-year inflation-indexed Treasuries were paying 4%, after inflation. Over the past 40 years, 10-year Treasuries have paid 2.73% over inflation, so inflation-indexed Treasuries (sometimes known as Treasury inflation-proof securities, or TIPS) may be very attractive at such prices.

APRIL 15

Tax Tip Treasuries' interest is exempt from state and local income tax, so these bonds are particularly appealing if you live in a high-tax jurisdiction.

However, inflation-indexed Treasuries should be held in a tax-deferred retirement plan because the annual inflation adjustment is subject to tax each year even though it's not paid in cash.

DIRECT ACTION

The Treasury Direct program allows you to buy Treasuries via a toll-free phone line (800-943-6864) or the Bureau of Public Debt's web site (www.publicdebt.treas.gov). The price will be deducted from a designated bank account so you don't have to bother mailing in forms or checks.

With this buy direct service you pay no fees, other than a $25 annual charge if your account exceeds $100,000. (Most brokers would charge you $50 or so to buy Treasury securities.) What's more, the minimum purchase for all Treasuries is now $1,000; before 1999 the minimums were $10,000 for short-term T-bills and $5,000 for intermediate-term T-notes.

BABY BONDS: EE SAVINGS BONDS

Another type of Treasury bond comes with a healthy helping of tax advantages: Series EE savings bonds. Savings bonds are available in denominations ranging from $50 to $10,000. Each bond's purchase price is equal to half of its face value; the bonds are redeemed at full face value on maturity.

EE savings bonds offer:

✔ *An inflation hedge.* If inflation accelerates, interest rates will move up. EE bond yields are adjusted every six months, so you'll enjoy higher yields.

✔ *Competitive yields.* Yields on savings bonds are 90% of the yield on five-year Treasuries. In late 1999, they were paying 4.3%.

✔ *Interest.* Interest is credited every month. Thus, you can cash in bonds without worrying about losing interest that you've earned. However, if you cash in EE bonds before a five-year holding period you'll lose three months' interest.

✔ *Low costs and convenience.* You can buy EEs at any bank for as little as $25. No commissions need to be paid to anyone.

A Taxing Choice

You have a choice as to when to pay federal income taxes on an EE bond investment. You may either (1) pay taxes annually, as interest accrues, or (2) pay taxes when you cash in the bond, when you transfer it to someone else, or when the bond matures.

No special form is needed to defer income tax on these bonds; all you have to do is hold on to your bonds and let the interest accrue.

In some circumstances, it makes sense to pass up the deferral. Suppose, for example, that you buy EEs for your newborn daughter Jane. She has little or no other investment interest.

On a tax return for Jane, you report the EE bond interest that accrues the first year and each year thereafter, paying no tax as long as she has scant investment income. Then she won't owe tax on that interest when the bonds are redeemed.

Learning to Love Tax Exemption

Furthermore, if EE bonds, purchased in the parent's name, are used to pay for a child's college tuition (and the parent is in an acceptable income bracket), interest earned can be completely free of local, state, and federal income taxes.

✔ EE bonds purchased after 1989 may qualify.

✔ They must be purchased and owned by parents, who must be at least 24 years old when buying the bonds.

✔ When redeemed, the interest must be used to pay college bills—tuition and fees—for a dependent child.

✔ At the time of redemption, the parents' adjusted gross income must meet certain tests. The income threshold increases each year: For 1999, parents get some break if their income is less than $110,000 on a joint return and, for tax-free interest, income must be under $80,000.

Holding Pattern

If you decide to invest in EE bonds, who should own them?

If you think you'll eventually qualify for the higher-education tax exemption described earlier, keep the bonds in your own name.

Otherwise, if you're buying EE bonds for a child, grandchild, or great-grandchild, register the bond in the youngster's name so the interest will be taxable to him or to her, not to you. This will usually generate the lowest income tax bill.

ROLL CALL

At maturity, you have the option of rolling over EE bonds into Series HH bonds, and again deferring the federal tax on the accrued interest until the HH bonds mature or are redeemed. (The present interest on the HH bonds is taxed each year.)

If you own U.S. savings bonds issued over 30 years ago, those bonds may no longer pay interest. The federal government doesn't send out notices to bondholders when interest payments cease.

It's up to you to cash in your old bonds or exchange them for HH bonds. Such an exchange maintains the tax deferral from your old savings bonds but the ongoing interest from HH bonds is currently taxable.

> **APRIL 15 municipal bond**
> an obligation of a state or local government agency. The interest paid is generally exempt from federal income tax and perhaps from other income taxes as well.

MUNIFICENT MUNIS

Treasury bonds offer safety from default and a refuge in times of crisis. On the other hand, if you buy bonds mainly for current income you probably will be better off owning high-quality tax-exempt (municipal) bonds. Such bonds have very little default risk so there's almost as much credit safety as there is with Treasuries.

What's more, the interest from *municipal bonds* (munis) is exempt from federal income tax. If you buy bonds issued within your state you'll probably avoid state income tax and even local income tax as well.

> **APRIL 15 general obligation (GO) bond**
> a municipal bond that is backed by all of the issuer's resources, which makes the risk of default unlikely.

> **APRIL 15 Tax Tip**   Municipal bonds should be held in a taxable account rather than a tax-deferred retirement plan; if you buy munis for your retirement plan you'll achieve the extremely undesirable result of converting tax-exempt interest to income that's fully taxed at your highest marginal rate.

Different Strokes

Municipal bonds are tax-exempt IOUs issued by public agencies, typically issued in units of $5,000.

> **APRIL 15 revenue bond**
> a municipal bond backed by the proceeds from a specific project, which means there is some risk investors won't be repaid.

Quite a variety of municipal bonds exists. For example, the issuer (state or local government) of a *general obligation (GO) bond* often uses this type of financing to build roads or schools and backs its GOs with its full faith and credit. The GO issuer is obligated to pay both interest and principal to investors out of the government's general revenue, which includes taxes.

Revenue bonds, on the other hand, finance public works where both interest and principal payments flow purely from revenue produced by the funded project.

Some municipal bonds are free of state and local taxes but do not avoid federal income taxes. These taxable munis, otherwise known as private activity bonds, are used to fund private projects such as industrial business parks or shopping malls. Since they are not usually triple tax-free, private activity bonds typically offer a much higher yield than their more traditional counterparts.

Zero Can Be a Plus

Municipal bonds are also available in the zero coupon format. Zero coupon municipal bonds are sold substantially below face value and deliver face value on maturity. The profit reaped at maturity is tax-free.

TAXABLE OR TAX-EXEMPT?

In order to make a fair comparison of a taxable versus a nontaxable investment, you must either calculate the after-tax return of the taxable investment or calculate the taxable equivalent of a nontaxable investment. To convert a nontaxable investment (such as a municipal bond) into its taxable equivalent, employ the following formula:

✔ First, determine your tax bracket. (For simplicity's sake, we will deal only with the federal rate here, but for triple tax-free munis, your combined federal, state, and local tax rate should be taken into consideration.)

✔ Second, subtract that bracket amount from 1. For example, if you are in the 28% tax bracket, subtract 0.28 from 1, which equals 0.72.

✔ Third, divide the yield of your nontaxable investment (perhaps a muni yield of 5%) by 0.72 (or whatever number was produced by the second step above): 0.05 divided by 0.72 equals 0.069 or 6.9%.

According to this formula, in a 28% tax bracket the taxable equivalent for your 5% tax-free yield would be 6.9%. You would have to invest in a taxable investment (such as a corporate bond) yielding more than 6.9% in order to achieve a better return than that offered by your municipal bond investment. (Taking state and local taxes into account would make the nontaxable investment even more attractive, assuming you invest in a local issue).

Pocketbook Issue

After-tax, high-bracket investors will receive more spendable income with munis. Even if you intend to reinvest rather than spend your bond interest, your net cash flow probably will be greater with munis.

Suppose, for example, AAA-rated municipal bonds maturing in 10 years are yielding 5% while 10-year Treasuries pay 6%. A taxpayer in a 36% bracket would net only 3.84% with the Treasury bond while someone in the top 39.6% bracket would get to keep a paltry 3.624%. Obviously, your after-tax income would be much higher with 5% munis.

If your tax bracket is moderate, you won't gain as much from buying munis. That is, a 28% bracket investor would net 4.32% from a 6% Treasury, 0.68% less than the return from a 5% muni. For that difference—$68 per year on each $10,000 invested—you might prefer the liquidity and crisis protection of Treasuries.

A MATTER OF MATURITY

If you decide on munis, you need to decide whether to buy short-, intermediate-, or long-term bonds. Opting for a longer term in the muni market (e.g., 30-year maturities) might earn higher yields but the extra yield doesn't seem worth the extra risk.

That is, if interest rates go up sometime during the next 30 years, your bonds would be devalued. You have much less interest-rate risk with shorter-term bonds.

CONCERN OVER CALLABLES

Munis are not *liquid*—they're costly to buy and sell—so investors who buy them should hold until maturity.

Unfortunately, that may not always be possible. Many municipal bonds have a *call feature* that allows issuers to redeem them before maturity.

Therefore, you should be wary of paying premium prices for high-coupon munis. Although the yields may be tempting, chances are they'll be called in prematurely and you'll wind up with a capital loss.

 liquid
an asset is liquid if it is easily salable at a market price.

call feature
the right, held by some bond issuers, to pay off bondholders before maturity, at a preset price.

FUND FAULTS

Many investors, once they decide to invest in munis, choose municipal bond mutual funds. According to Morningstar, Inc., Chicago, there are over 1,800 muni funds from which to choose, and those funds have attracted over $300 billion worth of investors' dollars.

Nevertheless, muni funds might not be your best choice. When you invest through a mutual fund you'll have to pay a fee, and those fees likely will be substantial. In 1999, Morningstar reported that the average expense ratio for municipal bond funds was 1.04%: Investors were paying over 1% per year in fees while the underlying assets (the bonds) were yielding around 5%.

Those expenses eat into investors' returns. (The average yield from municipal bond funds was 4.4% at that time, while higher yields were available to investors who purchased munis directly.)

DIRECT APPROACH

Does it make sense for investors to bypass the intermediaries and purchase municipal bonds outright, rather than through funds? That's the course advocated by some professionals. Many individuals appreciate the control they get from buying their own bonds.

Once you have a certain amount to invest you can purchase municipal bonds from various issuers and thus reduce the risks of holding only a few bonds. Investors can buy municipal bonds in pieces as small as $5,000, so for a $50,000 outlay you can have 10 different issues.

Setting the Standards

credit quality
the likelihood that the issuer of a bond will live up to its obligations.

When you buy munis you'll probably want a certain *credit quality* and a certain maturity. Once you set those parameters, you may not care which city's bonds you wind up with.

In terms of credit quality, most investors buying individual bonds should seek the highest-rated issues. Municipal bonds are rated by agencies such as Moody's Investors Service and Standard & Poor's, with the top ratings AAA, AA, and A.

Sure Things

The higher the quality of the bond, the more efficient the market and the more suitable for individual investors. Insured municipal bonds typically can be purchased with minimal commissions; they benefit from efficient markets, and they require little or no credit research.

insured bond
an obligation that carries private insurance. In case the issuer is unable to repay investors, the obligation shifts to the insurance company.

Insured munis are liquid, too, so they can be sold if that becomes necessary. *Insured bonds* are backed by private insurance against default and typically carry AAA ratings.

A Staggering Success

If you decide to buy top-rated munis, which maturities should you prefer? One strategy is to stagger maturities out to five or even 10 years. Then, as each bond matures, the proceeds can be reinvested in a good spot on the yield curve, where the risk-reward ratio is favorable.

This strategy, known as laddering, reduces the interest-rate risk. That is, if interest rates rise and bond prices fall, you will redeem your bonds periodically and be able to reinvest at the new, higher rates.

With individual issues you know how much you'll receive and when you'll get your principal back; with a bond fund, you never know how your cash flow will fluctuate or whether you'll get a return of principal.

INFORMATION, PLEASE

You can get information about municipal bonds on the Internet. The Bond Market Association's web site (www. investinginbonds.com) posts end-of-day prices on about a thousand municipal bonds, collected by the Municipal Securities Rulemaking Board, available online the following morning.

For example, suppose you want an AAA-rated New York bond that matures in 10 years. At this web site, you'll see what other investors are paying for such bonds and what yields are being offered.

You can see how much extra yield you'd earn stretching maturities from 10 years to 20 years, or by going from an AAA-rated to an A-rated bond. If your broker offers you a bond, you'll be able to tell if the price is reasonable (that is, if the yield is competitive) by comparing it with the prices of similar bonds in recent trades. The more information that's disseminated, the more efficient muni markets will become and the greater your chance of finding a fair deal.

A FAREWELL TO MUNIS

Bond investors naturally gravitate toward municipal bonds. Why own Treasury bonds or bond funds paying, say, 6% if you're in a high tax bracket?

If you stretch for yield with corporate bonds or bond funds, the interest is subject to federal, state, and local tax as well, which will drop your after-tax yield even lower.

Instead, you can buy muni bonds or funds (in-state munis, if you live in a high-tax state). You'd keep all the tax-exempt interest.

That strategy probably makes sense while you're working. But after you retire and begin collecting Social

Security, think again. Your tax bracket might drop, reducing the advantage of owning munis. If you're in a 15% tax bracket in retirement, you'd net about the same from Treasuries that you'll receive from munis. Moreover, Treasuries are safer and more liquid than munis.

AN UNHEALTHY COMBINATION

provisional income

an amount derived to determine if Social Security benefits will be taxable. To calculate provisional income you add your adjusted gross income, your tax-exempt interest income, and one-half of your Social Security benefits.

What's more, municipal bond income and Social Security benefits don't mix well. Your Social Security benefits may be taxed heavily depending on the amount of your *provisional income*, which is the total of your:

1. Adjusted gross income (AGI),
2. Tax-exempt interest income from municipal bonds and municipal bond funds, and
3. One-half of your annual Social Security benefits.

For example, with AGI of $18,000, tax-exempt interest income of $6,000, and $14,000 in annual Social Security benefits, your provisional income is $18,000 + $6,000 + $7,000 = $31,000.

On a joint return, you can have provisional income up to $32,000 without having to pay any tax on your benefits; for single filers the threshold is $25,000. Over those amounts, up to 50% of your benefits can be taxed, and if your provisional income is greater than $44,000 on a joint return or $34,000 filing singly, up to 85% of your benefits will be taxed.

As you can see, tax-exempt income gets the same weight in this formula as taxable earned or investment income. Thus, your municipal bond income is effectively taxable—it contributes to your paying higher taxes on Social Security benefits.

ANALYZING THE ALTERNATIVES

If you're a retired or almost-retired municipal bond investor, sit down with your tax preparer and crunch some numbers. See how much benefit you get from your municipal bonds or bond funds, if you're receiving any real benefit at all.

What are some of your options?

If you don't need the cash flow, consider switching from munis to fixed annuities (see Chapter 10). You may get a higher yield and the untaxed buildup won't cause your Social Security benefits to be taxed.

If you do need the income, consider shifting into Treasuries or corporate bonds, where the yields are higher than muni yields. After-tax, you might come out ahead.

As another alternative, shift money into stocks or stock funds and withdraw cash as needed by selling shares. By adroit portfolio manipulation you can sell shares at a taxable loss or at a gain taxed at 20% (even 10%, if your retirement income is modest). The money you don't withdraw can stay in stocks, where you may get the benefit of untaxed appreciation.

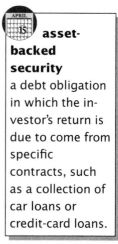

mortgage-backed security
a debt obligation in which investors receive mortgage payments that have been made by property owners, usually home-owners.

asset-backed security
a debt obligation in which the investor's return is due to come from specific contracts, such as a collection of car loans or credit-card loans.

OUTER REACHES OF THE BOND MARKET

There's more to the bond market than Treasuries and munis. Aggressive investors might stretch for yields in *mortgage-backed securities*, *asset-backed securities*, and perhaps junk bonds.

Mortgage-backed securities such as Ginnie Maes (they're issued by the Government National Mortgage Association, or GNMA) are popular; Ginnie Maes are backed by the federal government so there's very little risk of default.

Eyeing Ginnie Mae

Ginnie Maes, which are sold by most brokers, are mortgage pass-through securities. In essence, investors step into the shoes of mortgage lenders, collecting payments from borrowers.

In terms of interest-rate risk, Ginnie Maes are comparable to 10-year Treasuries yet they offer higher yields: They might pay 200 *basis points*—two percentage

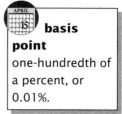

basis point
one-hundredth of a percent, or 0.01%.

points—more than Treasuries. They're backed by the full faith and credit of the U.S. government so they offer an appealing combination of liquidity, credit quality, and yield.

Singing the Refinancing Blues

The problem with mortgage-backed securities is similar to the one facing high-coupon municipal bonds: If interest rates fall, homeowners will refinance and investors will have to reinvest at lower rates. Investors who paid premium prices may lose money. Also, investors have to reinvest all payments of mortgage principal to avoid spending down principal.

Some of these problems can be avoided if you buy Ginnie Maes trading at or near par. If you don't pay a premium you won't lose money because of prepayments. There is little incentive for a homeowner with a 7% mortgage to refinance until mortgage rates drop sharply below that level.

In addition, you can buy securities that are backed by old mortgages that have yet to be refinanced. Mortgage holders who did not take advantage of previous periods of low interest rates are unlikely to do so. Thus, you're likely to lock in relatively high yields.

Stretching for Yield

Besides mortgage-backed securities, there are other alternatives to Treasury and municipal bonds. Corporate bonds, including convertibles and junk bonds, likely will generate higher long-term returns that Treasuries. They work best if held for the long term, in tax-deferred accounts so the interest won't be taxable each year. (The same is true for mortgage-backed securities.)

Extremely high yields may be available among closed-end bond funds, which trade like stocks, often at a discount to the value of the underlying securities. Closed-end junk bond funds were yielding over 10% in 1999, while closed-end emerging markets funds were yielding up to 20%.

If you're averse to investing in junk bonds or emerging markets bonds, consider multisector funds, which hold U.S. government, junk, and foreign government bonds. As a group, they've been stable; over time, the high current yields offered by junk bonds and foreign bonds likely will help to provide higher returns than you'd receive from a typical government or corporate bond fund.

Again, there may be greater opportunities on the closed-end side. Some closed-end funds have long histories of paying 8% to 12% yields, with large amounts of U.S. Treasuries in their portfolios. Closed-end multisector funds, too, belong in tax-deferred retirement accounts where distributions can compound, undiminished by annual income taxes.

Chapter

Making Mutual Funds Less Taxing

F inding information about mutual funds is not difficult these days. Virtually every business and financial publication reports on funds, providing past
performance data.

However, for many investors, this data is not accurate. The data assumes all distributions are reinvested, but
no adjustment is made for taxes. As a result you may
make poor investment decisions, based on inaccurate information.

OFFICIAL VERSION

Suppose Joan Jones invests $10,000 in ABC mutual fund,
buying 1,000 shares at $10 each. By year-end, the fund
sells for $15 per share. The fund makes an income distrib-
ution of 30 cents a share and a capital gains distribution
of $3 per share. (The $3 capital gains distribution reduces
the share price from $15 to $12.)

Joan reinvests all of these distributions ($3.30 per
share, or $3,300 on her 1,000 shares) in more shares of
ABC, now selling at $12. Thus, Joan buys 275 new shares,
bringing her total up to 1,275 shares.

total return
an investment's income return (interest, dividends) for a given time period plus or minus price appreciation or depreciation, realized or not.

According to the official statistics, Joan now owns 1,275 shares selling at $12, so her ABC holdings are worth $15,300. Compared with her $10,000 investment, Joan has a *total return* of 53%.

REALITY STRIKES

When it comes time to file her tax return, though, Joan will have to report $300 in dividend income and a $3,000 capital gain. Assuming a 40% tax rate (state and federal) on her dividends and a 24% rate on the capital gains, Joan will owe $840 in tax on those distributions, even though she hasn't touched a penny of them.

The bottom line is that Joan's true total return for the year is $4,460 ($5,300 minus $840), for a 44.6% gain. Her actual return is reduced by more than 15%, because of taxes.

DIMINISHING RETURNS

Such taxes have become a painful fact of life for mutual fund investors. Morningstar, Inc., recently reported on 264 large value funds (funds that tend to buy stocks of large companies trading at below-market price-to-earnings ratios) holding $522 billion in assets.

Over the past 10 years, the average fund in this category averaged an annual return of 14.9%, which means $10,000 would have grown to about $40,000, assuming all distributions were reinvested.

tax-adjusted return
a mutual fund's total return, after certain assumptions for an investor's tax obligations are taken into account.

According to Morningstar, though, the average *tax-adjusted return* would have been only 12.2% per year, assuming top federal tax rates but no other income taxes. At that level, investors would wind up with approximately $31,600, not $40,000.

Therefore, on a $10,000 investment in the average fund in this category, $8,400 would have been lost to taxes over 10 years. Over longer time periods, the tax bite may be even crueler, reducing paper returns by 30% or even 40% after 15 or 20 years.

SPREADING THE PAIN

It is true that such calculations are based on the highest federal tax bracket and not many investors will be in the top bracket, which applies only to taxable income in excess of roughly $290,000. In a lower tax bracket, the cumulative loss to taxation would be reduced.

On the other hand, the analysis does not include state income taxes, which apply to investors in 43 out of 50 states. The relative impact of state taxes is actually often more pronounced for moderate-income investors. No matter what your tax bracket, you're likely to lose control over your personal finances when you buy mutual funds in a taxable account. The annual tax bite can add up to a huge amount over the years.

Making a Difference

The numbers just mentioned are averages. There are large variations from fund to fund, which can make a big difference to investors. For example, Salomon Brothers Investors Fund outperformed MSDW (Morgan Stanley Dean Witter) Value-Added Portfolio over the 10 years at issue, 16.2% to 13.8% in annual total return. After-tax, though, the MSDW fund actually did better, 13.0% to 12.3%.

PLAYING BY THE RULES

The laws on mutual fund taxation explain such discrepancies. In order to avoid the corporate income tax, mutual funds must pass through to shareholders virtually all their (1) dividend and interest income, as well as (2) profits on sales of securities.

✔ Dividends and interest are taxed as ordinary income. For most stock funds, this isn't a significant problem because dividends are low these days.

✔ Short-term capital gains on securities held one year or less also are taxed at ordinary rates. This can be expensive for investors in funds that trade their portfolios actively.

✔ Long-term capital gains are taxed no more than 20% at the federal level. After the bull market of the 1980s and 1990s, many funds have sizable gains; when they sell appreciated shares investors might face serious tax consequences.

Such gains are taxable to investors even if the distributions are reinvested in the same fund, which typically is the case. Thus, mutual fund investors are likely to be taxed each year on "gains" they've never actually received.

PERFORMANCE PAYOFF

The aforementioned rules may be of little concern to mutual fund managers who generally are rewarded for their pretax rather than their after-tax return. Therefore, most managers trade without regard to the tax consequences for investors.

How can you invest in mutual funds yet avoid paying hefty taxes? Look for funds you think will perform well, pretax. Among those on your short list, favor the following types of funds, because they are likely to deliver the highest after-tax returns:

✔ *Tax-managed funds.* An increasing number of funds are designed specifically to trim investors' taxes. They offset gains with losses or they sell high-basis shares when reducing a position in a given company.

✔ *Low-turnover funds.* Some funds do relatively little trading, which means fewer gains to pass through to investors. For example, the tax-efficient MSDW Value-Added Portfolio mentioned earlier has had turnover rates from 11% to 19% in the past few years while Salomon Brothers Investors Fund has posted turnover rates up to 86%.

✔ *Index funds.* *Index funds* are designed to track a particular market index, such as the S&P 500. They seldom realize taxable gains because the makeup of the index stays fairly constant. Thus, they make few trades and they don't have many taxable gains to pass on to investors.

 index fund
a mutual fund with a goal of matching a specified index rather than beating the market.

> **APRIL 15**
>
> **Tax Tip**   Even if you invest in a tax-efficient fund, you may owe substantial amounts of tax if you switch among funds frequently. The best way to reduce taxes is to trade funds sparingly.
>
>   What's more, buy-and-hold investors generally wind up with better pretax returns than traders.

THE PAST CAN'T PREDICT THE FUTURE

Just because a fund has been tax-efficient in the past does not mean it will continue to be tax-efficient. Some funds have high tax efficiencies as a result of excellent performance and the resulting cash inflows. If performance sags, cash may flow out, leading to redemptions and capital gains distributions.

Moreover, a mutual fund may change managers and the new manager may not continue its tax-efficient investment policy. In fact, a new manager may dispose of older, appreciated holdings, triggering all the deferred gains at shareholders' expense.

Therefore, mutual funds that have had high tax efficiencies may someday generate unforeseen tax bills. You may prefer funds that are intentionally tax-managed and thus likely to maintain a superior degree of tax efficiency.

COMPLEMENTS ARE WELCOME

Many investors take a "hot fund of the month" approach to buying mutual funds. They wind up with a collection of funds, not a truly integrated portfolio. Over the long term, you're likely to be better served by holding funds meant to complement each other.

How can you build a well-balanced mutual fund portfolio? U.S. stocks should be the core of your portfolio. Over every extended time period in this century, U.S. stocks have delivered excellent returns to investors, so that's where most of your money should be.

STICK WITH STOCK FUNDS

Your stock market participation will depend a great deal on your age and your risk tolerance. In your 30s and 40s, with decades of investing in front of you, stocks might comprise nearly all of your investment portfolio. If you can stand sharp declines such as those that rocked the market in 1973–1974 and 1987, you might as well own stocks for their long-term returns.

Older investors probably should hold fewer stocks but should not leave the market entirely. You might hold 50% to 75% of your portfolio in stocks at age 65, depending on your risk tolerance, and switch 1% from stocks to bonds each year.

Go Global

Once you have a stock market allocation, there is one more decision you need to make: Should you include the stocks of foreign countries? Most advisers recommend some foreign stocks in your portfolio. If U.S. stocks hit a prolonged slump, there's a chance that international stocks will do better.

TOTAL RETURNS

Suppose, for example, you decide that you're comfortable with a portfolio consisting of 75% in stock funds and 25% in bond funds; of your stock funds, you want 60% of your assets in domestic funds plus 15% outside the United States. At this stage, there are several ways to go about fund picking.

The simplest way is to buy a total stock market index fund. Some funds are managed to track the Wilshire 5000, an index that covers virtually the entire U.S. stock market. In general, index funds have low expense ratios, which is a real advantage for investors. Buying a total market index fund gives you an easy way to cover the entire domestic market.

SMALL WONDERS

Not every investor believes in this one-size-fits-all approach. If you invest in an index fund, you'll wind up with the index's returns, and many investors seek above-average returns. What's more, total stock market funds tend to be about 70% weighted in large-capitalization (*large-cap*) stocks. Many investors prefer a higher portion of their assets in *small-cap* stocks, which have provided better long-term results than the large-caps.

You may decide, for example, to split your portfolio evenly between the stocks of large companies, which have proven records, and small companies, which have the potential for explosive growth. Assuming you want this 50–50 split, you have to decide which funds to use to fill each role.

ACTIVE OR PASSIVE?

For large-caps, the basic choice is an index fund: The evidence is overwhelming that it's hard to go wrong using an index fund for large-cap stocks. Index funds have low expenses because they hold down transactions; managers aren't jumping from one stock into another. What's more, low-turnover index funds tend to generate smaller tax bills for investors.

Even if you decide to use an index fund for large-cap stocks, there's no obligation to index your small-caps; the case for indexing is a lot weaker once you go beyond the S&P 500. A first-rate portfolio manager may have more opportunities to pick winners among small-cap stocks and thus beat index funds.

One strategy, then, is to combine an S&P 500 index fund with an actively managed small-cap fund. However, how can you tell whether a fund is a small-cap? Morningstar classes hundreds of funds as small-caps, including many that have "small-cap" in their name, but also many that don't.

large-caps stocks that have the greatest market capitalization; that is, their outstanding shares have the most value among publicly traded stocks. Generally, the most widely-known U.S. companies are large-caps.

small-caps publicly traded stocks with relatively small market values. (Notice the word "relatively"— some small-caps have market values up to $1 billion.)

Source Material

You can find out by doing some research. Many business publications indicate mutual fund categories; other sources of information are available at libraries or on the Internet. The key is to find out whether the fund really holds small-caps in its portfolio.

Always ask to see a fund's prospectus before investing, and read what it has to say. You'll be able to learn about the fund's investment philosophy and see what stocks it's actually holding.

Of course, you may not want to stake half of your stock market participation on one fund's manager, who might pick technology stocks when health care becomes the fashion. Spreading your bets can reduce this risk but you shouldn't overdo it. Generally, one or two well-selected funds in each asset class should be all you need.

Going in Style

Picking two funds instead of one won't help much if both managers pick the same types of stocks. One way to overcome this problem is to adopt a style-specific approach to stock picking. For example, if you want two small-cap funds, you might pick one *value fund* and one *growth fund*.

Another strategy you can follow is to simply read up on funds and send for several prospectuses. Try to pick two funds with complementary rather than identical approaches, then check on their past performance to see if you're truly buying diversification.

For example, Baron Asset Fund and Delaware Trend Fund are both considered *mid-cap* growth funds by Morningstar and both have solid performance records, but their patterns differ. Delaware Trend, which owns smaller companies, has had some great years (up 50% in 1989, 74% in 1991, 43% in 1995) but also losses of 25% in 1990 and 10% in 1994. Baron Asset never returned over 35% in any one year, but it hasn't had a loss since 1990. In 1994, when Delaware Trend lost 10%, Baron Asset gained over 7%. In 1998, when Baron Asset barely gained 4%,

value fund
a mutual fund that specializes in buying stocks that seem low-priced compared to the overall market.

growth fund
a stock fund that buys companies with outstanding prospects for increasing earnings.

mid-caps
stocks that are too big to be small-caps yet not sizable enough to be large-caps.

Delaware Trend returned nearly 14%. Thus, combining these two funds might give you one that zigs when the other zags, and vice versa.

A FOREIGN FLAVOR

Beyond domestic stocks, you might want to add some international stocks to your portfolio. Here, you have to decide whether you want just developed nations (Japan, Western Europe) or if you want emerging markets as well. You can buy one fund that will span the world or several different specialty funds, depending on how much fund picking you're willing to do.

GETTING A FIX ON FIXED-INCOME

Once your equity slots have been filled, you can go on to fixed-income funds. You likely will prefer municipal bond funds for tax-exempt income; if you're in a high-tax state, you may prefer in-state muni funds. For bond investments inside your retirement plan, you can choose taxable funds.

When you pick bond funds, low expenses are critical to long-term performance, so that's what you should look for.

Don't overload on funds. Most investors need no more than a dozen funds, spread among all the various asset classes. That's enough to provide diversification yet it's not too many to monitor.

A TAXING DILEMMA: INSIDE OR OUT

Besides buying too many funds, a common mistake is to neglect tax ramifications. You likely have investments both inside and outside of tax-deferred retirement plans.

Assuming you do most of your investments in mutual funds, you need to decide which fund goes where. Putting some thought into your mutual fund portfolio can reduce the IRS's share while providing more for you and your loved ones.

✔ Funds that have a history of making sizable capital gains distributions should be held inside your plans, where you can reinvest those distributions without having to pay tax on them each year.

✔ If you invest in municipal bond funds, never hold them in a tax-deferred account. You'll convert tax-exempt interest to taxable interest when you pull money out of the plan.

✔ Your cash reserves should be kept in a money market fund (perhaps a tax-exempt money market fund) outside of your plan. This will increase your access to these funds.

✔ If you invest in taxable bond funds, including junk bond funds, hold them inside your plan. The plan will provide shelter for the high level of income these funds generate.

✔ Among stock funds, put the most tax-efficient funds outside the plan.

For example, the Schwab 1000 Fund tracks the Schwab 1000 Index of the largest public companies. Since its inception in 1991, the fund has paid out 1% to 2% per year in income dividends and never distributed any capital gains. (Turnover is virtually nil at this buy-and-hold fund.)

Holding this fund inside a retirement plan would be a mistake. Because it generates almost no taxable income each year, you'd be wasting your retirement plan tax shelter. Then, when you take money out of the fund, you'd pay tax at ordinary income rates up to 39.6%.

On the other hand, holding this fund outside of your plan means you'd pay almost no tax each year. Then, you'd owe only 20% on realized long-term capital gains.

Indeed, many index funds are good choices for your taxable accounts.

✔ In general, growth-oriented funds are more tax-efficient than value-oriented funds, while small-company funds are more tax-efficient than large-company funds. Thus, you'll probably want to hold small-company growth funds in your taxable account.

Moreover, small-company growth funds tend to be volatile. If they lose ground, you'll be able to sell them and use the tax losses to offset gains elsewhere, which you can't do with funds held in a retirement plan.

✔ Put the least tax-efficient funds in your retirement plans. The higher a fund's turnover rate and the greater its annual capital gains distribution, the better the fit inside a tax-deferred plan. For example, Fidelity Select Health Care Portfolio posted extraordinary returns throughout the 1990s. However, the fund has made "monstrous distributions" in recent years, according to Morningstar, so it's tax-inefficient and best held in a tax-deferred account.

✔ High-dividend stock funds (utility funds, real estate funds) belong inside a retirement plan, where the distributions can be sheltered.

✔ If you mix individual securities and mutual funds, hold the mutual funds inside your retirement plan, where capital gains distributions can be sheltered.

Surmounting the Tax Overhang

What's more, some funds have been deferring taxes for so long that they hold large amounts of appreciated stocks. You may want to hold such funds inside a retirement plan to protect yourself against the day when those gains are realized.

Therefore, before you invest in any fund you should do your homework. Find out about the fund's history in regard to distributions while you're learning about fund objectives, past performance, and manager duration.

PACKAGED DEALS

When you invest in mutual funds you have two basic choices. One, you can do your own research and choose your own funds, probably buying those that charge no sales loads. Two, if you don't feel up to selecting from among more than 10,000 funds you can rely on the help of a broker, a financial planner, or some other adviser.

There is definitely a need for objective investment advice and guidance in choosing mutual funds. However, many investors are growing leery of paying commissions. As a result, mutual fund *wrap programs* have emerged to provide investment advice for a fee rather than for a commission. Reportedly, about 70 mutual fund wrap programs hold more than $50 billion in assets.

wrap programs arrangements in which investors pay fees rather than sales commissions for investment advice. Typically, the fee paid is a percentage of the value of the assets in the account.

Pay As You Go

What are mutual fund wraps? In essence, they are investment programs in which you pay a fee based on the assets in the program. With a 1% fee—which is common— you'd pay $1,000 per year on a $100,000 account. If your account grows to $200,000, you'd pay $2,000; and so on. Thus, you don't have to worry about an adviser urging you to buy and sell funds in order to generate sales commissions.

For your fees, you can expect substantial services. Typically, you'll have an initial interview with a financial adviser. As part of this interview, you'll fill out a questionnaire designed to determine your goals and your risk tolerance. Your answers to the questionnaire will be fed into a computer program, which will classify you as extremely conservative, extremely aggressive, or somewhere in between.

Based on the computer scoring and the interview, an asset allocation will be determined. Typically, the younger you are and the greater your risk tolerance, the greater the stock market allocation. Older, conservative investors will be advised to tilt their allocations more toward bonds.

Asset allocation in these wrap programs usually does not stop at stocks and bonds. Instead, you might wind up with an allocation that calls for 20% in large-company growth funds, 15% in large-company value funds, 5% in small-company growth funds, 10% in corporate bond funds, and other categories, until the total reaches 100%.

FILLING THE GAPS

Once your asset allocation has been determined, your adviser will recommend specific mutual funds to use for each category. Generally, the sponsoring organization will have an approved list to choose from. Some wrap programs recommend up to five funds per category, based on past performance and interviews with the fund managers. You and your adviser might pick one or two funds per category; often, both load and no-load funds will be among the choices, with the latter made available without the usual sales charges.

Once the chosen funds are purchased, your adviser's responsibilities include ongoing monitoring and account rebalancing. You'll get a comprehensive statement, perhaps once a month, to show you how your funds are performing and to help with your tax planning. Each wrap program has a minimum account requirement; minimums range from $10,000 to $100,000, with $50,000 the norm.

Those are the basics but not all mutual fund wrap programs are alike.

✔ *Packaged wraps.* In these plans, the sponsoring firm has a certain number of model portfolios and each investor is matched with one of those models. If you work with a bank on a mutual fund wrap, you'll likely be in a packaged program. Naturally, mutual fund families offer wrap programs that tend to rely heavily on their own mutual funds.

✔ *Open wraps.* Such programs allow the investment adviser to generate asset allocations and pick funds. Thus, you're more likely to get a customized portfolio, but you're also more reliant on the talents of your particular adviser. Packaged programs, by comparison, offer portfolios put together by an internal investment committee.

Some wrap programs are hybrids of open and packaged programs. That is, each investor is assigned to a certain model portfolio. However, financial advisers are allowed to modify asset allocations for their clients and to substitute mutual funds, using selections from a preapproved list.

UNRAVELING WRAP PROGRAMS

Therefore, one factor to consider in evaluating mutual fund wraps is plan flexibility. As long as you have confidence in your adviser, you'll want a plan that's tailored to your individual needs.

What else should you look for?

- ✔ *A personal up-front evaluation.* Your adviser should make a thorough effort to discover your individual circumstances before recommending a portfolio.

- ✔ *Fair fees.* Wrap programs charge a fee that typically ranges from 0.5% to 2% of assets per year. Generally, that fee will be paid quarterly, transferred directly from your brokerage account to your adviser.

All of the fees you'll pay should be fully disclosed, in writing, and they should be easily identified on the statements you receive. Beware of wrap programs that charge other fees, such as deferred sales charges.

You also should determine which assets will be subject to fees, especially if you participate in a 401(k) or similar retirement plan. Many advisers will provide advice on how to choose among 401(k) options at no charge, because they're not actually managing that money. However, if you give your adviser your PIN (personal identification number) along with your permission to trade the funds within the plans, you can expect those assets to be included in the management fee.

- ✔ *Treatment of existing holdings.* You probably have a portfolio to begin with, when you sign up for a wrap program. If you sell everything, you may trigger a large tax bill. Thus, most advisers try to keep some of the existing assets, if possible, and build the rest of the portfolio around the retained holdings.

✔ *Consolidated reporting.* One reason to use a wrap account is to get one statement covering mutual funds from several different families.

✔ *Delineation of responsibility.* In recent years, large-company stocks have surged while small-company stocks have lagged. In some mutual fund wrap programs, large-cap funds will be sold automatically, replaced with small-cap funds, to bring the allocation back into line.

With other wrap programs, a meeting or a phone call between you and your adviser is mandatory whenever an allocation goes a few points off the recommended path so further strategy can be discussed. You may prefer a nondiscretionary wrap, where no funds are bought or sold without your consent.

EASING THE TAX BURDEN

In addition, a wrap program should take your tax situation into account when deciding which funds are to be sold. Suppose, for example, by the end of the year you have taken substantial capital gains. To offset these gains, your wrap program may suggest which funds to sell at a loss and which similar funds can be purchased to take their place.

Moreover, some wrap accounts will suggest which funds should be held inside an IRA or a qualified retirement plan and which should be held outside. Generally, high-turnover funds, which generate substantial income taxes, should be held inside a retirement plan.

COST CONTROL

Considering all of these factors, do mutual fund wraps make sense? Perhaps, if you rely on an investment adviser. You'll likely have a well-diversified portfolio and you'll avoid being churned (saddled with excessive sales commissions). Your adviser knows that asset-based fees will increase if your funds grow, so you both will have a strong incentive to build up your portfolio. Nevertheless, mutual fund wraps have a cost. In addition to the fees that you pay to the managers of your mutual funds, you'll have to pay a fee to your financial adviser each year. A 1% fee on a $700,000 portfolio, for example, would mean paying $7,000 per year.

If your portfolio is relatively stable, paying that much money each year may not be necessary. At some point, you may be able to negotiate a better deal, paying your adviser by the hour or a flat-fee annual retainer. The rap on wrap accounts is that they can become expensive, so you need to be vigilant about how much you're paying and what you're getting in return.

Real Tax Breaks from Real Estate

Your real estate may be your most valuable asset. If handled properly, it may also become a highly tax-advantaged investment. Familiarity with the real property tax rules discussed in this chapter should alert you to some of the tax breaks, as well as costly tax mistakes, associated with the purchase and sale of real property.

THE $500,000 HOME SALE EXCLUSION

Thanks to the Taxpayer Relief Act of 1997, you can avoid paying tax on gains up to $500,000 when you sell your house. To qualify for this break, you must be married when you sell the house you've lived in during two of the previous five years. (Single homeowners get a $250,000 exemption.)

For example, if you have a $100,000 basis in your home—money you've paid to buy and improve the house—you can sell it for up to $600,000 without owing anything to the IRS. Then, you can buy another house with that $600,000 and sell it for up to $1.1 million, tax-free, repeating the process as often as every two years.

Under previous tax law, there was a $125,000 capital gains exclusion you could use only once, after age 55. If you've used that exclusion, it doesn't matter now: You can sell your house and use the new tax shelter. That also is true if you've remarried to a spouse who has used the age 55 exclusion.

> **Tax Tip** There's a time to wait and a time to sell your house quickly. If you're about to get married, and both of you own homes, wait until after the wedding to sell one. You'll get a $500,000 rather than a $250,000 capital gains exemption. On the other hand, try to sell before you're widowed or divorced because your capital gain exclusion will drop from $500,000 to $250,000.

acquisition indebtedness
a loan secured by your house or by a vacation home, incurred when you build, buy, or substantially improve the property.

home equity indebtedness
a loan secured by a home but used for purposes other than building, buying, or improving the house.

MORTGAGE INTEREST DEDUCTION

Currently, the federal government allows homeowners to deduct from their income taxes the interest portion of their home mortgage payments. The mortgage ceiling (for purposes of determining deductible interest) on this *acquisition indebtedness* is at present set at $1 million.

The federal government also currently allows a deduction for interest paid on home equity loans. The aggregate amount of the loan (or loans), for purposes of calculating the interest deduction on this *home equity indebtedness*, is limited to $100,000.

SHIFTING INTO REVERSE

Home Equity Conversion Mortgages (HECMs), insured by the Federal Housing Administration (FHA), were created by the Department of Housing and Urban Development (HUD) in 1988 through a limited demonstration program of 2,500 mortgages, eventually expanded to

25,000 mortgages. The Federal National Mortgage Association (FNMA—Fannie Mae) expanded the market dramatically with its Home Keeper mortgage, introduced in 1996. Now, many banks offer *reverse mortgages*, which come in several forms.

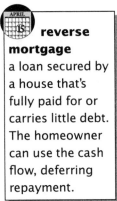 **reverse mortgage**
a loan secured by a house that's fully paid for or carries little debt. The homeowner can use the cash flow, deferring repayment.

Most popular are "lifetime mortgages," which will pay you as long as you live in the house or until you die. At that point, all the loan proceeds, plus accrued interest, will become due. If you choose this type of mortgage, be sure it includes a provision stating that the loan balance will never exceed the value of your home. Thus, the lender won't have any claim against your other assets.

To be eligible for most reverse mortgages, you must be at least 62 years old (that means both owners if the house is owned jointly). The house must be a single-family principal residence, owned free and clear or subject to a very low mortgage.

The greater the property's appraised value and the older you are, the larger the available loan. A single owner can borrow more than the joint owners because chances are the lender will get repaid sooner. Frequently, if you agree to permit the lender to share in future property appreciation, you can borrow more.

There are tax benefits, too. Money received from a reverse mortgage is considered a loan, so it's not taxable income. Loan proceeds won't reduce your Social Security benefits; neither will they count as income for the purposes of determining whether your Social Security benefits will be taxable.

VACATION HOME OPTIONS

Mortgage interest is deductible on a vacation home if you occupy it as a residence. That is, you must use it personally for more than 14 days out of the year, or more than 10% of the time that it is rented out.

If your vacation home is rented for fewer than 14 days per year, the entire mortgage interest is deductible (subject to the limitations noted). If your vacation home is rented for more than two weeks per year, but you meet

> **Tax Tip**   If you rent out your vacation home for no more than 14 days each year, not only can you deduct your mortgage interest, but the rental income received is tax-free—you don't even have to report it on your tax return.

the residence requirements, then the interest deduction is apportioned, based on the home's actual use.

In this situation, a fraction of your mortgage interest payment will be construed as a rental expense (and thus will be deductible to the extent of the gross rental income from the vacation home). The rest can be deducted as residential mortgage expense.

RENTAL REAL ESTATE

depreciation
a deduction for a noncash expense, the estimated wear and tear on property you own.

For taxpayers holding a minimum 10% ownership in rental property, substantial rental income can be sheltered through income tax deductions. The cost of rental properties can be written off via mortgage interest deductions and *depreciation* over 27.5 years for residential rental property, or 39 years for commercial rental property (depending on the date you purchased your property).

Residential rental property is defined in the tax code as "any building or structure if 80% or more of the gross rental income from such building or structure for the taxable year is rental income from dwelling units."

LEARNING TO LOVE LOSSES

If your adjusted gross income (AGI) does not exceed $100,000, and you pass the "active participation test," up to $25,000 in tax losses from rental property can be used to offset other ordinary income. This offset is phased out as adjusted gross income exceeds $100,000; it is completely eliminated at an AGI of $150,000. For example, if your AGI is $118,000 this year, you can deduct up to $16,000 worth of losses from actively managed property.

For individuals with AGI exceeding $150,000, deductions can be used only to the extent that rental income is received in that taxable year. For example, if your AGI is $200,000 this year and you have $10,000 in taxable rental income, you can use up to $10,000 worth of passive losses from another venture as an offset. Unused losses may be carried forward.

Generally, real estate professionals can use losses from one actively managed property to offset income from other sources, no matter what their AGI. Therefore, married couples filing jointly can use this tax break as long as either spouse is a bona fide real estate professional.

> **APRIL 15**
>
> **Tax Tip** Own investment property as a limited liability company (LLC) rather than outright. You'll enjoy limited liability, which may protect your personal assets in case someone slips and falls on your property. An LLC is extremely flexible, if you want to make special allocations to other investors, and it makes it easier for you to deduct any tax losses (see Chapter 12).

GO WITH THE FLOW

When you own investment property, the money you receive from tenants may not be fully taxable. That's because of depreciation, a noncash expense.

To see how this might work, suppose Ned and Nancy Jones are retired; they invest $100,000 in a house across town, which they rent out to tenants. They bought the house with a $20,000 down payment and an $80,000 mortgage.

Assume that their rental income is $12,000 per year and their total expenses (including mortgage interest) are $10,000. Thus, they have $2,000 of *positive cash flow*, in

> **APRIL 15**
>
> **positive cash flow** revenues from a venture such as rental real estate that exceed the out-of-pocket costs.

real estate parlance; that's a 10% return on their $20,000 down payment.

Moreover, Ned and Nancy also are entitled to depreciate the property. This is a complicated calculation because the house will be depreciated under one schedule, furnishings and fixtures will be depreciated under another schedule, and the land is not depreciable. It's likely, though, that they'll be entitled to about 4% depreciation, or $4,000 per year (4% of the $100,000 purchase price).

 Tax Tip In depreciating a rental property, it will pay to hire an experienced accountant who can help maximize this deduction.

That $4,000 worth of depreciation deductions will completely offset Ned and Nancy's $2,000 in positive cash flow. Thus, they won't have any profits to report and they won't owe any income tax. Their $2,000 in income is tax-free.

DEPENDING ON DEDUCTIONS

Moreover, since Ned and Nancy's $4,000 depreciation deduction exceeds their $2,000 rental income, it provides them with a $2,000 net loss on paper. This loss can be deducted from their other income. If Ned and Nancy are in an effective 40% tax bracket (counting federal and state tax), a $2,000 deduction will put another $800 in their pockets.

As mentioned, in order to qualify for this deduction their AGI can't exceed $150,000 per year. For every $2,000 that their AGI is below $150,000, they can deduct up to $1,000 in real estate losses, up to a maximum of $25,000 per year if their AGI is below $100,000.

In addition, to deduct this loss they have to actively manage the property. They don't have to fix the plumbing but they must be involved in decisions about tenant selection, capital improvements, and so on.

HAPPY ENDINGS

If you sell investment property after holding it for at least a year, any profits will qualify for favorable capital gains tax rates, now set at 10% or 20%. Leverage will make your investment returns even greater. Suppose, in our example, Ned and Nancy sell their investment property for $120,000 10 years in the future. That's a 20% gain in property value, but their $20,000 profit would represent a 100% gain on their $20,000 down payment. They'll owe only $4,000 in tax on their 20% gain, at a 20% capital gains rate.

Moreover, if their investment property appreciates, Ned and Nancy have another option: They can *refinance*. With a property valued at $120,000, they might find a lender willing to advance $96,000 (80%). This will enable them to repay their old $80,000 loan and put $16,000 in their pockets, tax-free!

It's true that they'll have more debt service to pay, with a larger mortgage, but higher rents will make this obligation easier to bear.

> **refinance**
> replace an old mortgage with a new (presumably less expensive) mortgage.

TAX BREAKS CAN HELP MAKE COLLEGE HOUSING AFFORDABLE

If you have teenaged children or grandchildren, a special type of rental real estate may be appealing: investing in near-campus housing. While providing a place for your youngster to stay, you can earn rental income, find tax shelter, and perhaps even turn a profit. Fortunately, tax benefits can make it easier for you to come out ahead. The key to this strategy is a working knowledge of the town where the student will go to college. In the spring of the child's senior year in high school, after the college selection decision has been made, visit the area specifically to evaluate real estate sites. Location is critical, and one block may be much more desirable than another block a short distance away.

On your visit, look for a house or condo located

within a few miles of the campus so you can rent to students. Choose a neighborhood where the tenants and their parents (who'll likely pay the rent) will feel safe.

Sturdy, Not Stylish

Your house or condo should be large enough to accommodate at least four tenants. The property should be structurally sound but it needn't be too elegant.

Once you decide on a property, find out how much rent you can reasonably expect to receive and what your expenses are likely to be. Then make a bid that will allow you to cover your costs with positive cash flow left over. As long as interest rates are at low levels, you'll probably want to make a relatively small down payment and carry a large mortgage.

After you close the deal on a property, you'll have to get it ready for occupancy. If it needs basic landscaping, painting, repairs, and so forth, hire your student to do the work. You'll get a deduction for the wages you pay while the young person likely will get some tax-free pocket money for use during the school year. (In 1999, a single taxpayer can have up to $4,300 in earned income and owe no income tax.) Moreover, the student will become familiar with the property and the neighborhood.

When you furnish the property for tenants, purchase cheap but durable furniture. Each room should have a bed, desk, chair, chest of drawers, and small bookcase. Buy these pieces from garage sales, through newspaper ads placed by people who are moving away, and so on. Don't worry if the furniture in each room doesn't match; most college students won't mind. You'll probably spend a few thousand dollars, but the expense will be deductible.

Spread the Word

While this process is under way, list your apartments for rent. During the spring and summer before your child's freshman year, students who already are enrolled at that college are selecting their housing for the coming year. You can reach these students with notices in the college housing office, ads in local newspapers, and flyers around the area. Charge rents comparable to other near-campus apartments, based on your research.

Even if the rental process is slow, don't accept any tenant out of desperation. Instead, insist on formal leases, co-signed by the student tenant and a parent. Check the parent's reference, from a mortgage holder or a landlord. Be sure to collect at least one month's rent as a security deposit (two months' rent is better).

One drawback to campus housing is the seasonality— June, July, and August may be slow. To handle this problem, insist on full-year leases with sublet rights, to give your tenants the chance of renting to summer school students. Consult with someone who has rental property experience, in order to draw up a lease that will protect you and your property.

Your student can be one of your tenants, assuming the college has no policy against living off-campus. This will save you paying the cost of room and board.

In addition, you can pay your child a modest management fee, perhaps $100 per month for collecting rents, maintaining the property, and so on. Again, you can deduct the payments while your student probably will pick up some tax-free cash.

Graduation Present

Your rental can continue until your student has finished at the college. Then, you can sell the property by running ads in the local newspapers, "Free college housing for your student." If you've fixed up the property so it's suitable for student rentals, you're likely to sell at a gain.

If you manage to buy well and run your operation smoothly, you may enjoy several benefits. Just saving the cost of your student's room and board for several years might put you ahead by $20,000 or $25,000. In addition, any positive cash flow from the monthly rents can offset part of the cost of sending your child to college.

AN EDUCATION IN HIGHER TAXATION

You also may enjoy tax deductions that can shelter rental income or, in some circumstances, provide a deductible loss. Depreciation, interest, management fees, condo association charges, operating costs, taxes, and insurance are all deductible for property owners.

As mentioned earlier, if your AGI is under $100,000 you can deduct up to $25,000 worth of losses per year. If you have up to $150,000 in AGI, you'll be entitled to smaller deductions. However, even if the AGI rules prevent you from deducting losses immediately, you can carry forward excess losses and deduct them when you sell the property, winding up the deal.

Moreover, trips to visit the college town may be deductible if your primary purpose is to check up on your investment property. Phone calls to your student may become business calls to your property manager. The better your records, the greater your chances of sustaining these deductions.

At the end of the day, if you sell at a profit, you'll enjoy low tax rates: 20% on long-term capital gains and 25% on *recaptured* depreciation. The smaller the down payment and the larger the mortgage, the more you'll profit if you catch the local real estate market at the right time.

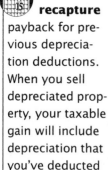 **recapture** payback for previous depreciation deductions. When you sell depreciated property, your taxable gain will include depreciation that you've deducted in the past.

Chapter

6

Super Real Estate Strategies

eal estate investors have to make some taxing decisions. When you sell investment property, you'll owe tax not only on any appreciation but also on the amount you've depreciated. In some cases, all the sale proceeds will be taxed.

Suppose, for example, you own an apartment building you bought many years ago for $600,000. Because you have fully depreciated the property, your basis in the building is now down to zero. You no longer want to own the building and you have a buyer willing to pay $1 million.

At first glance, you'd have a $400,000 profit (the $1 million selling price minus your $600,000 cost). At a 20% tax rate on long-term capital gains, you'd owe $80,000 to the IRS. However, your $600,000 worth of depreciation deductions also would be recaptured, at a 25% rate, adding $150,000 to your tax bill, for a total of $230,000. After paying off your mortgage and covering all the other costs, you might wind up with little in your pocket.

TRADE, DON'T SELL

Fortunately, there is a solution worth exploring: a *tax-deferred exchange*. In essence, you can swap one investment property for another without owing any tax.

Tax-deferred real estate exchanges are authorized under Section 1031 of the tax code. Such exchanges must involve investment properties (not personal residences) but the properties need not be perfect pairs. Your apartment building doesn't have to be exchanged for another apartment building; it may be swapped for a warehouse or a strip shopping center or any type of investment property.

If certain conditions are met, no tax will be incurred on the transaction. Indeed, if you hold on to the replacement property (or another property acquired in a subsequent exchange) until your death, your heirs will inherit the property with a step-up in basis to current value. They can sell the property they inherit and owe no income tax on any prior appreciation. (The property will be included in your taxable estate, however.)

The Indirect Approach

To exchange properties, you don't have to make a direct swap. Suppose, for example, Karen Shaw moves from Oregon to Ohio. She doesn't want to be a long-distance landlord but she wants to continue to own investment real estate.

In her situation, she can sell the property in Oregon, have the proceeds held by a third party, then use those proceeds to buy a replacement property near her new home.

Three for the Money

Indeed, most swaps today are multiparty deferred exchanges, often involving the services of a qualified intermediary, known as an *accommodator*. After you sell your original property, the proceeds go to the accommodator, who puts the money into an *escrow* account.

(Your relative or business associate can't serve as an accommodator.)

To protect your funds, you should insist that the accommodator provide a third-party guarantee, such as a *bank letter of credit*. The contract between you and the accommodator should state that this property transfer is one step in a planned exchange.

DON'T CUT CORNERS

In a tax-deferred exchange, it's extremely important to follow all the rules, especially those that involve timing. Otherwise, you can lose the tax deferral. You should retain a lawyer with extensive experience in this area, to make sure of qualifying for the tax deferral.

The timing rules on tax-deferred exchanges are explicit. After you transfer your property, you have 45 days to identify potential replacement properties, in writing, to the accommodator. Several properties may be identified, so you're covered in case an intended acquisition falls through:

✔ You can name up to three properties of any value; or

✔ You can name any number of properties with an aggregate value no more than 200% of the price you received for your property.

You have 180 days from the time you relinquish your property to actually close a deal for replacement property. In case you transfer your property after October 15 of any calendar year, the second deadline is actually April 15 of the next year, when your personal income tax return is due, but you can get the full 180 days by requesting an automatic extension of your personal income tax return.

After you have finalized the replacement purchase, the accommodator uses the money held in escrow to buy the replacement property. You've disposed of one property

bank letter of credit a document guaranteeing payment of a customer's obligations up to a stated amount for a given time period.

and acquired another, but you've never touched any cash, so capital gains taxes are deferred.

SWAP STRATEGIES

Tax-deferred exchanges can take other forms. You might, for example, have the buyer who wants your property purchase the replacement property instead. Then you can swap properties directly. Other exchanges may be much more complex, involving multiple parties.

Although property exchanged pursuant to Section 1031 must be "held for business or investment purposes" it is possible to convert a principal residence into an eligible property by first vacating the property and then holding it out for rental purposes for one to two years. Thus, if handled properly, the gain from a personal residence can also be rolled over into income-producing real property, without taxable recognition of that gain.

It's also possible to exchange for a property you'll want to use yourself. You might, for example, exchange investment property for a rental condo in an area where you plan to retire. Because the condo is now investment property, no tax will be incurred. In the future, when you retire, you can convert this condo to personal use without triggering the deferred taxes.

CRITICAL CRITERIA

In all cases, though, three criteria must be met in order for all taxes to be deferred:

1. The amount you pay for the replacement property must be at least as much as the price you receive for the property you relinquish.
2. All the cash you receive must be reinvested in the new property.
3. Any debt relief must be replaced by a combination of new debt and additional cash put into the deal.

Property Swap Kicker

The way the math works, if you meet the first two requirements, you'll meet the third one as well. If you wind up with net cash or a lower mortgage, you'll owe tax on that income, which is known as *boot*.

Suppose you sell your old property for $500,000, after all related costs. After paying off a $100,000 mortgage, you net $400,000 in cash. You buy a new property for $525,000, using the $400,000 as a down payment and taking out a $125,000 mortgage. Because you have received no cash and have a larger mortgage, you meet all the requirements for a tax-free exchange.

On the other hand, if you buy the property for $475,000, with $400,000 in cash and a $75,000 mortgage, you'd have a $25,000 taxable gain because of boot, in the form of a reduced mortgage.

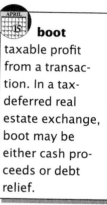

boot
taxable profit from a transaction. In a tax-deferred real estate exchange, boot may be either cash proceeds or debt relief.

PAYING THE PRICE

As you'd expect, tax-free exchanges are not cost-free. You'll likely have to work with a tax professional as well as an accommodator, who'll receive either a flat fee (perhaps $1,000 or more) or a percentage of the transaction. Therefore, you must weigh all the costs versus the value of the tax deferral.

Tax Tip   The more heavily mortgaged your property is, the more attractive a deferred exchange may be. That's because a large portion of the sale proceeds would go to debt repayment, leaving you with less to pay the IRS.

BANK BARRIERS

In some cases, property swaps run into roadblocks created by banks. You might need to add cash to acquire the replacement property, especially if you're paying off a mortgage on your original property. If so, you're likely to ask a bank or other lender for a mortgage.

Increasingly, banks in these transactions are worrying that you—the property owner—will run into financial difficulty and declare bankruptcy. In such situations, the replacement property may fall under the bankruptcy court's jurisdiction and the bank will lose its collateral for that loan. Therefore, some lenders are requiring property owners to set up a special-purpose entity (generally, a corporation) to buy and own the replacement property, in order to get such loans. Loans will be made only to such an entity, in hopes that it won't be dragged into a bankruptcy filed by the property owner.

Damaging the Deferral

That may be fine for the bank but not for you, the property owner. Because a different taxpayer (the special-purpose corporation) winds up owning the property, there's no tax-deferred exchange: You'd owe whatever tax would be triggered by a sale.

Not only would you owe tax on the deal, you'd wind up holding investment real estate property in a corporation, which is generally a poor strategy. Most investment property is owned outright, or by a partnership, to permit pass-through of depreciation deductions.

Getting around the Roadblock

To avoid such problems, instead of a corporation you can set up a single-member limited liability company (an LLC in which you're the only owner). Single-member LLCs are ignored for income tax purposes. Thus, if your single-member LLC owns the new property, it will be the same as if you had owned it outright, as far as taxes are concerned. (See Chapter 12 for more on LLCs.)

You'll be eligible for a tax-free exchange and for the pass-through of any losses. On the other hand, the LLC will be the property owner, not you. The lender likely will be assured that such a property can be kept out of bankruptcy, even if you become insolvent.

However, some states tax single-member LLCs as corporations. If you face this problem, try a grantor trust instead. Again, a *grantor trust*—a trust in which the grantor is treated as the owner of the capital and income interests—is ignored for income tax purposes. Thus, you can get tax-free exchange treatment for investment property while the lender gets the necessary security.

TAX CREDITS REDUCE YOUR TAXES, DOLLAR FOR DOLLAR

Another prime real estate tax shelter involves a *tax credit* for low-income housing. Tax credits provide tax savings by reducing the taxes you owe. Unlike deductions, tax credits are applied after your total tax bill has been calculated; at that point, tax credits reduce your tax obligation dollar for dollar.

If you help to provide housing for low- and moderate-income tenants, you can qualify for a tax credit. You can earn this credit on your own, but you're probably better off in a *limited partnership*, relying on the *general partner* to buy several properties in different areas and deal with all the requirements.

Tax Tip The IRS has been taking a hard look at properties claiming these credits. You need to invest in a partnership with a good general partner to keep the units rented to eligible tenants.

Trusty Tenants

Don't be put off by the name. Low-income housing doesn't mean no-income housing in big-city slums. Most partnerships buy properties located in small towns and rent units

grantor trust
a trust that generates income that's taxable to the trust creator rather than income reported on the trust's tax return.

tax credit
a direct reduction of a tax obligation.

limited partnership
a partnership in which some parties enjoy protection from the venture's obligations.

general partner
a partner who does not enjoy limited liability and so is fully exposed to the partnership's obligations.

to retirees or workers with modest incomes. The properties tend to hold their value.

Low-income housing (LIH) tax credits are spread over 10 years. Often, the period will stretch to 11 or 12 years because it may take some time for a partnership to invest all of its capital.

Long-Term Lock-In

Under legislation passed in 1993, tax credits are prefunded, attached to a property for the full time period. Congress can't change the rules in the middle of the game and rescind the tax benefits.

What kind of a return can you expect from these deals? Tax credits are estimated at 12% per year. Thus, if you invest $10,000 in an LIH partnership, you can expect about $1,200 worth of tax credits per year, once the partnership is fully operational. Altogether you can expect $12,000 in tax reduction for a $10,000 investment, over 10 to 12 years.

Making a Good Deal Even Better

Thus, you'll likely come out ahead from the tax savings alone. Considering the time value of the extra cash flow, these projected tax savings are equivalent to a 7% annual after-tax return. If you get your money back at the end of the deal (probably 15 years after you invest) your effective return will be about 12%, after-tax.

If your partnership sells its properties at a profit (perhaps to another tax credit partnership), your after-tax return will be higher; the same may be true if the properties are refinanced and proceeds distributed to investors.

Corporate Cash Cow

These partnerships are even better if you invest through a regular C corporation. Such corporations can deduct *passive losses*, which increases returns. (For most individual investors, deductions for passive losses must be deferred until the end of the deal.)

passive losses

real or paper losses from investment property or from an active business in which you don't participate. In many cases, such losses are not deductible right away.

Real Shelter for Retirees

If you're retired, there may be other advantages to investing in tax credit partnerships:

1. The credits are not considered earned income, so Social Security benefits won't be reduced.

2. The credits aren't considered income at all, so receiving them won't expose your Social Security benefits to income tax. By contrast, investing in tax-exempt municipal bonds may expose your Social Security benefits to income tax.

TAX CREDITS: NOT TOO MUCH OF A GOOD THING

Do these credits seem too good to be true? The federal government thinks that's the case, so there are limits as to how much individuals can effectively invest.

You probably can use enough credits for a $25,000 *deduction equivalent*. If you're in the top 39.6% federal tax bracket, you probably can use up to $9,900 in affordable housing tax credits per year ($25,000 times 39.6% equals $9,900). Thus, you can effectively invest up to $82,500 in a partnership ($82,500 times 12% equals $9,900).

If your tax bracket is lower, you're restricted to fewer tax credits. In a 28% bracket, for example, you're probably limited to $7,000 worth of credits per year ($25,000 times 28% equals $7,000), so you shouldn't invest more than $58,000 ($58,000 times 12% equals $6,960).

Of course, you don't have to invest $50,000 or more. Most tax credit partnerships have a $5,000 minimum.

> **deduction equivalent**
> the amount of tax a deduction will save you, in a certain tax bracket. In the 36% bracket, for example, a $25,000 deduction saves $9,000 ($25,000 times 36% equals $9,000).

Complicating Factors

If you have passive income from other sources, perhaps from rental properties that generate taxable income, you likely can invest more in affordable housing than the limits just described. On the other hand, if you deduct losses from actively managed investment property, you'll be eligible for fewer credits.

Suppose you deduct $8,000 this year from a rental property. Now, your deduction equivalent is $17,000 ($25,000 minus $8,000). In a 36% tax bracket you can use up to $6,120 worth of credits ($17,000 times 36%) by investing no more than $51,000 (12% of $51,000 equals $6,120).

What if you invest more than these upper limits? You won't be able to use all your tax credits right away. Unused credits can be carried backward three years or forward up to 15 years, perhaps to the end of the deal.

Dealing with the Downside

Another catch: LIH credits can't offset the alternative minimum tax, or AMT (see Chapter 16). Before you invest, check with your tax pro about your AMT exposure. You might find that you can invest only so much before running into the AMT.

Illiquidity may be a problem, too. Be prepared to buy and hold for 15 years. Even though your investment is transferable, if you need to cash out early you may not receive full value for your partnership interest.

The greatest risk in an LIH partnership is investing with an inept *sponsor*. You'll want a general partner who can verify tenant eligibility, handle all the paperwork, and provide investors with clear reports.

Check on a sponsor carefully before investing; ask to speak with other investors who have at least five years of positive experiences to relate.

sponsor person or company organizing a venture such as an investment partnership. In another context, an employer who offers a retirement plan to employees.

NO-SWEAT REAL ESTATE

You don't have to buy a rental property or invest through a limited partnership to own real estate. Real estate investment trusts (REITs, which rhymes with treats) allow you to buy investment properties as easily as you buy stocks.

Real estate investment trusts are companies formed to invest in real estate; many REITs own multiple properties. Under the tax code, a REIT that distributes at least 95% of its income owes no corporate income tax. Thus, REITs tend to distribute large amounts to investors.

Tax-Favored Cash Flow

What's more, some of those distributions may be tax-sheltered by depreciation deductions. An investor receiving a 7% distribution might pick up only 5% or 6% taxable income. (If so, the untaxed 1% or 2% is deducted from your basis, raising the tax you'll owe on sale, but the effect is to defer income and to shift highly taxed ordinary income to lower-taxed capital gains.)

Besides high yields, REITs offer liquidity. Most REITs trade publicly, like stocks, so investors can cash out whenever they want. The properties owned by REITs generally are managed by experienced professionals.

If you're interested in REITs you can buy individual issues selectively. Another option is to invest in a real estate mutual fund that holds REITs extensively. According to Morningstar, in 1999 there were 128 real estate funds holding over $9 billion in assets. These funds gained more than 30% in 1996, on average, and a further 22% in 1997, only to lose 16% in 1998.

Although REIT prices likely will fluctuate sharply from year to year, over the long term returns to investors will reflect the values of the properties owned by each REIT. Therefore, holding a portion of your investment assets in REITs. REIT funds can help to diversify your portfolio.

Chapter

Winning the Tax Deferral Game

ension plans and *individual retirement accounts (IRAs)* offer tax-deferred growth on investment assets. They also provide protection against financial perils resulting from illness, aging, and even death.

Retirement plans are governed by a complicated, often confusing area of law. Nonetheless, in order to get the most out of your retirement plan, you need to understand the contribution and distribution rules.

individual retirement account (IRA) earnings are not taxed, but the account must be emptied within a given time period and withdrawals are usually taxed.

IRAs PUT THE "I" INTO INVESTING

An IRA is an individualized retirement account, opened with an IRS-approved *custodian*, such as a bank, savings and loan, credit union, or brokerage firm. An IRA (established at a bank, for example) operates much like a regular savings account.

Other than the contribution and withdrawal limitations unique to an IRA (discussed shortly), the primary difference between an IRA and a regular savings account lies in the fact that the bank, as custodian, follows a different reporting process in tracking the owner's tax-deferred income for the government.

custodian a financial institution that holds assets for investors. Those assets may be inside of a tax-deferred retirement plan.

As a result, the annual fees charged are likely to be higher than those charged for a regular savings account. (To compensate, some banks will credit a slightly higher interest rate.)

THE $2,000 ANNUAL TAX BREAK

Contributions to an IRA are typically limited to $2,000 annually per worker, and $2,000 per worker's spouse. Under certain circumstances, set forth in the tax code Section 219, your IRA contribution is tax-deductible.

(Such circumstances include requirements that the account owner be $70\frac{1}{2}$ years of age or younger and have an adjusted gross income under certain levels. In most cases, a nonworking spouse will be able to deduct IRA contributions.)

> **APRIL 15**
>
> **Tax Tip**   Even if you qualify for an IRA deduction, you can wait until April 15 to make your contribution for the prior year.

Although you probably can contribute $2,000 per year to an IRA, whether that contribution will be deductible is a different matter. Generally, IRA contributions won't be deductible if you're an active participant in an employer-sponsored qualified plan and your income tops $40,000 ($60,000 on a joint return).

A spouse who does not participate in an employer's retirement plan can get a full deduction if joint adjusted gross income (AGI) is $150,000 or less. Smaller deductions are permitted up to $160,000 in AGI.

Suppose you're covered by your employer's plan but your spouse is a homemaker. In 2000, your AGI is $154,000. Your spouse isn't covered by an employer plan, so a deduction is permitted. However, because your joint AGI is 40% through the phaseout range ($150,000 to $160,000), your spouse's IRA deduction is limited to 60% of $2,000, or $1,200.

Unfortunately, taking money out of an IRA can be a taxing experience. If you fund your IRA strictly with deductible contributions, every penny that you withdraw is taxed at your regular rate by the IRS and perhaps by state and local tax collectors as well.

What if some or all of your IRA contributions were nondeductible? Then some or all of your IRA withdrawals will not be included in your taxable income. However, you need to keep exquisite records, perhaps for decades, to support your claim of tax-free withdrawals. The paperwork burden may not be worth the effort.

THE MAGIC OF TAX-DEFERRED COMPOUNDING

All IRA funds invested with an IRS-approved custodian will grow tax-deferred. As demonstrated by Figure 7.1, tax deferral is a powerful investment tool.

As you can see, a series of 30 $2,000 IRA contributions can grow to over $200,000, assuming a 7% investment return and a 28% federal income tax bracket. That's more than $60,000 greater (an additional 45%) than the

	IRA[1]	Taxable Investment[2]
5 years	$ 12,307	$ 11,671
10 years	29,567	26,473
15 years	53,776	45,469
20 years	87,730	69,759
25 years	135,353	101,063
30 years	202,146	140,537

FIGURE 7.1 Approximate Return— IRA versus Taxable Investment

[1]Investing $2,000 per year and in the 28% tax bracket.
[2]Assuming 7% annual yield in the 28% tax bracket.

buildup of those same 30 $2,000 investments in a taxable account.

Of course, a 7% investment return is actually fairly conservative. If you achieve greater returns, long-term, the advantage of tax-deferred compounding will be even more pronounced. Similarly, the higher your income tax break the more you will benefit from tax deferral.

Start Now

Not surprisingly, the sooner you can take advantage of tax-deferred growth, the better. As Figure 7.2 shows, the cost of waiting can prove to be significant.

If you invest $2,000 per year at ages 22 through 29, the $16,000 you invest in those years will compound to a significantly greater amount than $72,000 invested over the next 36 years, from ages 30 through 65!

ROTH IRAs: TAX-FREE, NOT JUST TAX-DEFERRED

Roth IRA
an IRA that offers no deductions for contributions but which may provide tax-free withdrawals after five years and age 59¹/₂.

The Taxpayer Relief Act of 1997 tax law created a new type of IRA, the *Roth IRA*. Now you can contribute up to $2,000 per year to a Roth IRA instead of (not in addition to) a regular IRA. Roth IRA contributions are not deductible, but, in certain circumstance, all of the earnings and the withdrawals can be tax-free.

To qualify for tax-free withdrawals, you can't draw out the earnings from a Roth IRA until you reach 59¹/₂ years of age. If you start your Roth IRA when you are older than 54¹/₂ you must wait at least five years before withdrawing earnings.

Exception: Earnings of up to $10,000 may be withdrawn at any time to help with a first-time home purchase, tax-free.

When you take money out of a Roth IRA, you are taking out contributions first (in the eyes of the IRS), then earnings. Withdrawals of contributions don't count as taxable income.

Suppose you start your Roth IRA at age 35 and decide to retire after 20 years of $2,000 contributions, at 55.

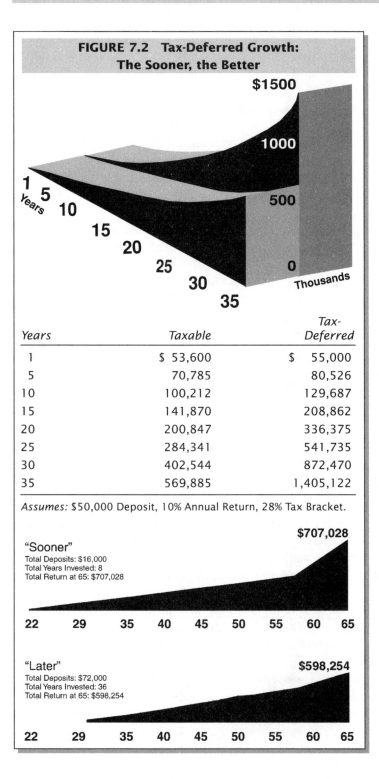

FIGURE 7.2   Tax-Deferred Growth: The Sooner, the Better

Years	Taxable	Tax-Deferred
1	$ 53,600	$ 55,000
5	70,785	80,526
10	100,212	129,687
15	141,870	208,862
20	200,847	336,375
25	284,341	541,735
30	402,544	872,470
35	569,885	1,405,122

Assumes: $50,000 Deposit, 10% Annual Return, 28% Tax Bracket.

$707,028

"Sooner"
Total Deposits: $16,000
Total Years Invested: 8
Total Return at 65: $707,028

| 22 | 29 | 35 | 40 | 45 | 50 | 55 | 60 | 65 |

"Later" $598,254
Total Deposits: $72,000
Total Years Invested: 36
Total Return at 65: $598,254

| 22 | 29 | 35 | 40 | 45 | 50 | 55 | 60 | 65 |

You're not yet 59$^{1}/_{2}$, so you won't qualify to withdraw earnings tax-free. You can, however, withdraw up to $40,000—the amount you've contributed over the years—and owe no tax or penalties. Then, when you reach age 59$^{1}/_{2}$, you can withdraw the earnings, too, tax-free.

To contribute the full $2,000 per year to a Roth IRA, your adjusted gross income can't exceed $95,000 on a single return, $150,000 on a joint return. Partial contributions are allowed up to $110,000 (single) or $160,000 (joint). Taxpayers with greater incomes are ineligible for Roth IRAs.

For many people, a Roth IRA will beat a deductible IRA. The more years you have until retirement and the higher your anticipated retirement tax bracket, the greater the advantage of a Roth IRA.

If you're covered by a *401(k) plan*, one strategy is to defer just enough of your salary to get a full employer match (assuming there is an employer match), then contribute $2,000 to a Roth IRA, assuming you meet the income test. Your Roth IRA contribution is not deductible but you may enjoy tax-free withdrawals in retirement.

 401(k) plan
a retirement plan in which employees elect to defer part of their salary. The deferred amounts are invested and no tax is due on the investment income until withdrawal.

 education IRA
an IRA that provides tax-free withdrawals if used to pay higher-education bills.

LEARNING ABOUT EDUCATION IRAs

Although IRA stands for individual retirement account, the *education IRA*, a creation of the 1997 tax law, can't be used for retirement. Instead, contributions must be made on behalf of children 18 and under while the payouts must be made for college expenses.

As long as the money comes out of an education IRA for higher education costs, no taxes will be due. However, contributions are nondeductible and they can't exceed $500 per student beneficiary per year. Contributions on behalf of a particular student can't be made in the same year that student receives contributions for a prepaid tuition plan, which are available in many states.

The income limits are the same as they are for Roth IRAs: To make the maximum $500 annual contribution you must have AGI below $95,000 on a single return or $150,000, filing jointly. Smaller contributions can be made up to $110,000 and $160,000 in AGI, respectively.

The income limits are not really meaningful because anyone can contribute to an education IRA for your kids. Suppose, for example, that Joe and Jan Smith earn $175,000 per year so they're over the limit. Joe's mother is a retiree whose income is under the limit so she's allowed to contribute $500 per year to her grandchildren's education IRAs.

MIXED BAG

Generally, any investment is appropriate for an IRA, with the noted exceptions of collectibles (paintings, for example), commodities, and leveraged investments (such as mortgaged real estate).

However, investments that are typically sought after for their tax-advantaged status (such as municipal bonds) lose much of their allure when owned by an IRA. All income (even otherwise tax-exempt income) is taxable when withdrawn from an IRA.

A REAL-LY DIFFERENT IRA INVESTMENT

For long-term investing, loading up your IRA with stocks and stock funds usually makes sense. However, there's no guarantee that stocks will rise forever. If the market treads water for a time or even sinks, you may be glad that you've diversified your retirement fund. Therefore, if you're extremely knowledgeable about real estate, you may be confident you can achieve excellent returns by putting some of your IRA money into real estate.

If you do intend to invest IRA money in real estate, you're probably better off not putting the properties themselves, or any portion of a property, into the account.

Inside the IRA, the tax advantages of real estate are lost. You can't take depreciation deductions, you can't deduct paper losses, and you can't take advantage of long-term capital gains. Every dollar that comes out of your IRA will be taxed as ordinary income, even if that money comes from selling real estate at a profit.

In addition, under federal law, you can't hold mortgaged property in your IRA. Without leverage, you're giving up your best chance for sizable property profits.

Thus, you're better off investing in properties in a personal, taxable account rather than in your IRA.

LOAN ARRANGERS

If you shouldn't hold property in an IRA, how do you invest in real estate? Through real estate–related debt. In essence, your IRA is allowed to lend money to a borrower who'll use the proceeds for a real estate venture, just as your IRA is allowed to buy Treasuries (that is, lend money to the U.S. government) or certificates of deposit (lend to your local bank).

When it comes to making real estate loans, here are some activities to consider:

✔ *First mortgage loans.* In many situations, the returns on *first mortgages* will be substantial. You can charge points, too; this effectively raises the interest rate even higher.

✔ *Second or third mortgage loans.* The interest rates you'll receive for a *second mortgage* or a *third mortgage* will be higher than prevailing first mortgage rates. Again, you can charge points.

✔ *Participating mortgages.* In a *participating mortgage*, you'd share in the profits—if any—of the property owner. You might, for example, structure a loan to pay either a minimum interest rate or 25% of the owner's gains, whichever is greater.

✔ *Options.* You might purchase a *property option*. If the property is sold during your option term, the seller must buy your option back, giving you a handsome profit.

 first mortgage
a loan secured by real estate. The holder has the first claim on the property in case of a default.

 second mortgage
in case of default, lenders who make second mortgage loans can collect only after the holder of the first mortgage is paid in full.

 third mortgage
holders of third mortgages come after the holders of first and second mortgages if a borrower defaults.

BORDERLINE BORROWERS

If you are interested in making IRA real estate investments, keep in mind that your borrowers likely will have questionable credit ratings. If they were top-rated, they'd simply go to the bank or tap their own funds for the money they need.

Therefore, careful checking is a must. Look hard at the borrowers in the specific transaction before handing out any money from your IRA.

Moreover, the loans you make should be formal, drafted with the advice of a professional adviser. A secured loan, bearing a realistic interest rate, will help protect you from a challenge that your IRA engaged in illegal activity while also shielding you from borrowers who might not live up to their promises.

Impact: Considering the risks you're taking and the amount of work that's involved, you should expect to earn at least 15% on such deals, on an annualized basis, with the opportunity for even higher returns.

participating mortgage
a loan that entitles the lender to a share in any future property appreciation, in addition to interest.

property option
the right to acquire real estate during a certain time at a specified price.

TAXING SUBJECTS

On the tax side, if your IRA gets involved in real estate you should be certain it's making a true loan and thus not entering into a prohibited transaction. In addition:

Don't make any loans involving yourself, your relatives, or business entities in which you have a substantial interest. Even if the loan is made on realistic terms and your IRA stands to benefit, such *self-dealing* is forbidden.

Get all real estate loans valued by a knowledgeable, unrelated party. The assets in your IRA must be valued at certain times, in order to calculate required minimum distributions and the tax on Roth IRA conversions. Such valuations may be expensive, which is yet another reason to set deal terms so you'll wind up with significant returns.

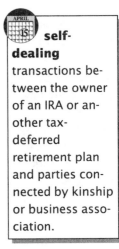

self-dealing
transactions between the owner of an IRA or another tax-deferred retirement plan and parties connected by kinship or business association.

CULTIVATE A CUSTODIAN

All of these concerns won't matter unless you can find a suitable entity to serve as trustee and custodian for a self-directed IRA. Major brokerage firms probably won't be interested. Your best bet may be to seek out a local bank or trust company, perhaps one that you've dealt with over the years as a real estate investor.

There's no reason that a financial institution can't serve as a trustee if your IRA holds real estate–related paper, but most firms won't want to get involved because they'll have to go beyond routine tasks. Search for a cooperative custodian before you line up any deals.

PENSIONS PAY OFF

Pension plan variations abound, and each plan has its own specific contribution limit.

A 401(k) plan allows employees to direct a portion of their salaries into a special investment account. In many 401(k)s, the employer then matches each employee's contribution with its own contribution. For example, for every dollar the employee adds, the employer might contribute 50 cents. An employee's contribution limit to a 401(k) for 2000 is $10,500.

defined benefit plan a tax-deferred retirement plan designed to pay a certain retirement benefit based on earnings and years of service.

Defined benefit plans pay a fixed retirement benefit, which is usually calculated as a percentage of the employee's average salary over the last few years prior to retirement. If the set percentage is 50%, for example, and the employee's final salary averages out to $100,000, the annual retirement benefit might be $50,000 (depending on contributions made and the actual earnings on those contributions).

Annual contributions are calculated based on the present value of what will yield the anticipated future benefit. Traditionally, older, highly paid employees have benefited from this type of plan, particularly if they needed to speed up funding in the later years. However, in 2000, contributions are based on a salary cap of $170,000.

Defined contribution plans focus on the size of the annual contribution (as opposed to the ultimate benefit).

A company might contribute a fixed percentage of an employee's salary (perhaps 10%) each year to a type of defined contribution plan known as a *money purchase plan*.

Alternatively, a *profit-sharing plan* allows a company to decide, from year to year, how much to contribute. The annual contribution limit for either type of defined contribution plan is $30,000.

Simplified employee pensions (SEPs) are similar to defined contribution plans in that contributions are made based on a percentage of an employee's earnings. The SEP differs, however, in one important respect: There is no general plan. Rather, each participant has his or her own individual IRA to which the company contributes. (Other dissimilarities include the SEP's immediate vesting and eligibility requirements, and annual contribution flexibility.)

Annual contributions to a SEP are limited to 15% of an employee's pay, per year, up to a current maximum of $24,000. SEPs have been popular retirement vehicles due to their administrative simplicity.

SIMPLE plans, created by the Small Business Job Protection Act of 1996, may be used by firms with 100 or fewer employees. They can be structured as IRAs for self-direction, or as 401(k)s in which participants pick from a menu of investment choices.

SIMPLE plans require little paperwork. There's no *nondiscrimination testing*, so employers can maximize contributions to their own accounts regardless of whether any employees elect to participate. Contributions to any individual's account can't exceed $12,000 per year (in 2000), including a 100% employer match. SIMPLE plans require employer contributions on behalf of employees.

---

defined contribution plan
a tax-deferred retirement plan in which the ultimate payout depends on how well the contributed funds are invested.

money purchase plan
a type of defined contribution plan that requires employers to contribute certain amounts each year.

profit-sharing plan
a type of defined contribution plan in which employers can contribute varying amounts each year.

simplified employee pension (SEP)
a tax-deferred retirement plan requiring little paperwork.

SIMPLE plan
a low-paperwork retirement plan (savings incentive match plan for employees) available to employers with no more than 100 employees.

nondiscrimination test
calculation designed to ensure that an employer-sponsored retirement plan benefits most employees, not just top management.

FORTIFY YOUR 401(k) WITH AN EMPLOYER MATCH

Most employers offer 401(k) or similar retirement plans. They allow you to defer some of your income (and the income tax) until you retire. The deferred earnings can compound tax-free over the years.

What's more, many employers encourage 401(k) participation with matching contributions. Commonly, employers offer a 50% match of employee contributions up to 6% of salary.

For example, suppose Karen Brown earns $50,000 per year. If she contributes $3,000 (6%) to her 401(k) account, her employer will contribute $1,500.

Therefore, you always contribute at least enough to get the full employer match. Otherwise, you're passing up free money.

If possible, go beyond 6% to 8%. (In many 401(k) plans, you're permitted to make larger, unmatched contributions.) The extra two points ($1,000 per year for Karen in our example, about $20 per week) won't be missed, yet those two points may make a huge difference over decades of tax-deferred compounding.

The Roth Revision

An alternate approach mentioned earlier in the chapter is to make 401(k) contributions up to the employer match, then contribute $2,000 to a Roth IRA. The latter contribution is not deductible but you may enjoy tax-free withdrawals in retirement.

Set the Proper Pace

If you contribute the current maximum ($10,500) annual salary deferral to your 401(k) plan, don't get there too rapidly. You might forfeit some matching contributions.

Suppose you earn $120,000 per year and you participate in a 401(k) plan that will match contributions 50%, up to 6% of pay. Thus, you should be able to receive a $3,600 match on a $10,500 contribution (50% × 6% × $120,000 = $3,600).

However, if you contribute $1,050 per month, the $10,500 maximum will be reached after 10 months. Your employer will contribute $300 per month for a $3,000 match, leaving a $600 shortfall.

Tax Tip Instead of $1,050 per month, contribute $875 per month for 12 months. Your employer will match $300 per month for 12 months, bringing the annual match to the expected $3,600.

KNOW WHERE TO HOLD 'EM

After deciding how much to contribute to your 401(k), you have to determine how to invest your money, dividing your contribution between stock funds and yield-paying investments (bond funds, money market funds, etc.).

✔ The younger you are, the higher the percentage of your assets that should be in stock funds.

✔ Although most of your stock funds should hold U.S. blue chips, you should include some small-company and international stock funds for diversification.

✔ Always read a mutual fund's prospectus before committing 401(k) money. Try to find funds with complementary styles; it makes no sense to own three funds that all hold General Electric, Coca-Cola, and Gillette.

Cost Cutter

When you select funds, lean toward funds with low expense ratios, as revealed in the prospectus. Low turnover rates can lead to low transaction costs. Over time, such economies can increase your returns dramatically.

A Matter of Semantics

Some 401(k) plans offer a choice among several balanced portfolios. That is, an aggressive investor might choose a portfolio with 70% in stocks and 30% in bonds while a conservative investor might prefer 50% or 60% in bonds. The portfolio manager takes responsibility for keeping the desired balance.

Don't confuse such balanced portfolios with asset allocation accounts, also available in some 401(k) plans. In the latter accounts, asset allocations will move, based on the manager's judgment. That is, a professional adviser will attempt to time the market, going from stocks to bonds and back as market conditions indicate.

BORROWING TROUBLE

Many 401(k) plans allow participants to borrow from their accounts. You can get a hassle-free loan and pay yourself back, with interest.

However, such loans are repaid with after-tax dollars; then you'll pay tax again when you withdraw money from your account. Thus, 401(k) loans expose you to double taxation.

In addition, if you leave your company, any outstanding loan needs to be repaid. If you can't repay, the loan will be treated as a distribution, subject to income tax and possibly a penalty before age $59\frac{1}{2}$.

The bottom line? You should use your 401(k) plan as a lender of last resort. If you need money, and bank loans aren't available, a 401(k) loan is better than a credit card loan with interest rates up to 21%.

SPREADING THE WEALTH

Many 401(k)s offered by publicly held companies include employer stock on the menu. No matter how bright you think your employer's prospects are, you should avoid having too much of your portfolio exposed to just one stock.

Thus, if you have a choice, keep your investment in employer stock down to no more than 10% of your 401(k) holdings.

In some cases, your employer will match your contribution with its stock rather than cash. What's more, you may be restricted from selling any of that stock before age 50, for example.

If so, sell the stock as soon as you can to get down to (or even below) the 10% mark. Don't take risks with your retirement because of misplaced loyalty.

COMPANY STOCK WINDFALL

As indicated, employees of publicly owned companies frequently accumulate company stock in their tax-deferred retirement plans. When such employees leave the company and roll their plan balance into an IRA, they have another option to consider.

Instead of rolling the company stock into the IRA (or selling the shares and rolling the proceeds), the company stock can be withdrawn from the plan.

Why would you want to do this, in such a situation?

First, you'd owe income tax right away, but only on your basis in the shares. That is, if the shares in the plan were valued at $50,000 when acquired by the plan, you'd owe tax on $50,000 worth of ordinary income. That's true even if the shares are now valued at $500,000.

The second reason is that eventually, appreciation can qualify for capital gains treatment. In this example, the *net unrealized appreciation (NUA)* would be $450,000. Upon sale of the shares, the NUA would

net unrealized appreciation (NUA) paper profits on company stock withdrawn from a tax-deferred retirement plan. Eventually, a sale of this stock may qualify for favorable long-term capital gains treatment.

qualify for the 20% rate on long-term gains, assuming certain holding period requirements are met. Subsequent appreciation, too, could qualify as a long-term gain.

Daunting Dilemma

This tax break, appealing as it is, presents taxpayers with a difficult choice:

1. Hold on but risk exposure. If you continue to hold on to the NUA stock ($500,000 worth, in this example), you'll probably have a large portion of your net worth tied to the fate of one company. A break in the stock price could cost you $100,000 or more in a few days.

2. Sell the shares and pay the tax. If you dispose of some or all of the shares, to reinvest in other securities, you'll owe tax on the deferred gains. Selling the shares might have the same effect as a 10% or 20% market break.

3. Roll the shares into your IRA, where you can sell them and reinvest the proceeds. This approach gives you diversification and tax deferral but you'll owe ordinary income tax on all the money as it's withdrawn.

Sweet Charity

 charitable remainder trust (CRT) a trust that pays a specified amount to you or the other beneficiaries you name yet eventually will pass to a charity or charities you choose.

A 1999 IRS letter ruling (9919039) suggests a possible solution to this quandary:

1. You can withdraw the NUA stock from the retirement plan.

2. The NUA stock can then be contributed to a *charitable remainder trust (CRT)*.

3. The trustee can sell the NUA stock and reinvest in a diversified portfolio.

4. You (and perhaps your spouse) can be income beneficiaries of the trust, receiving lifetime payouts based on the full value of the securities.

5. Ultimately, the trust fund will be distributed to a charity or charities.

Contributing NUA stock to a charitable remainder trust is not specifically permitted by the tax code. Therefore, a letter ruling was requested. In its response, the IRS ruled:

✔ Other plan assets may be rolled into an IRA, tax-free. If there is a trustee-to-trustee transfer, no withholding will be required.

✔ No ordinary income tax will be owed on the NUA of the withdrawn stock.

✔ A subsequent sale of the NUA shares will qualify for capital gains treatment.

✔ The 10% penalty for early withdrawals will not apply to the NUA stock, if the taxpayer is over 55 and truly has separated from service from the employer sponsoring the plan.

✔ The transfer of the withdrawn NUA shares to a charitable remainder trust won't trigger a tax obligation.

✔ Income and gift tax deductions will be available, based on the current market value of the shares transferred to the charitable remainder trust.

✔ No tax will be triggered if the trust sells the donated NUA shares.

✔ Income paid out by the CRT will be taxed in the normal manner of income from such trusts, so a sizable portion of the income may be taxed at capital gains rates.

Thus, this two-step plan (withdraw NUA stock, contribute the shares to a charitable remainder trust) preserves the tax deferral and the capital gains treatment of the NUA. What's more, your retirement fund will be diversified, not tied to one company's stock.

As an added benefit, you likely would be entitled to a sizable up-front tax deduction.

In general, this strategy makes sense for individuals who have a large block of stock (at least $250,000 worth) and a high retirement tax bracket. Otherwise, the expense involved in creating and maintaining the trust won't be worthwhile.

In addition, be prepared to spend as much as $20,000 up-front to get a letter ruling from the IRS. Strictly speaking, you don't need a ruling, but it's certainly prudent to get one.

SOCIAL SECURITY: UNCLE SAM'S RETIREMENT PLAN

Social Security is the government's answer to the retirement, disability, and survivorship needs of the American worker and his/her family. The program is funded through contributions made by both employees and employers.

As in most qualified pension plans, contributions made by the employee to Social Security are not taxed at the time of contribution. Also like qualified plan benefits, Social Security benefits are taxed at the time they're received.

Up until recently, Social Security benefits had more favorable tax treatment. Unfortunately, the Omnibus Budget Reconciliation Act (OBRA) of 1993 changed the rules, subjecting up to 85% of Social Security benefits to federal income taxation.

How large a tax bite will be taken from your Social Security benefits depends on your provisional income: If you are single, and have provisional income from $25,000 to $34,000, 50% of your benefits will be taxed. Provisional income exceeding $34,000 triggers 85% taxation of benefits. For married couples filing jointly with provisional income of $32,000 to $44,000, benefits are subject to 50% taxation, while provisional income above $44,000 triggers the 85% tax.

Provisional income is defined as the sum of adjusted gross income, nontaxable interest income (such as interest from municipal bonds), and half of your Social Security benefits (see Chapter 3).

You can receive Social Security retirement benefits as early as age 62. However, those benefits will be reduced by 20% of what you would have received had you waited until age 65. Spousal entitlements are also reduced, if early retirement is taken, from 50% to 37.5%.

On the other hand, if you retire after age 65, you can receive greater benefits. For each additional year you work from age 65 to age 70 you can receive an additional 4.5% to 8% in benefits, depending on your date of birth.

Working after retirement can also affect your Social Security benefits. For example, if you are younger than 65 and earn annually more than $10,080 (in 2000), your benefits will be reduced by $1 for every additional $2 earned. If you are between 65 and 69 and earn more than $17,000 (in 2000), your benefits will be reduced by $1 for every additional $3 earned. However, if you are 70 or older you can earn any amount without penalty.

Chapter

Employers Can Take
Their Pick of the Pack

I f you're an employer, your age, your income, and your type of company will determine what plan works best for you. The ever-changing tax laws will also likely impact your choice of retirement planning vehicle.

For example, pursuant to the Omnibus Budget Reconciliation Act (OBRA) of 1993, the annual eligible compensation limit (for the purpose of calculating qualified retirement plan contributions) is $170,000 in 2000. This eligible compensation limit impacts the nondiscrimination test for 401(k) plans, and will limit maximum annual deferral for a SEP to $25,500 and defined contribution plans to a $30,000 annual contribution limit. Defined benefit plans can allow even greater annual (deductible) contributions.

Nonetheless, whether you participate in a defined benefit plan, defined contribution plan, 401(k) plan, or SEP, your invested dollars will grow tax-deferred. Needless to say, tax-deferred growth is preferable to the alternative.

Not only annual contributions to but also withdrawals from pension plans and IRAs must be planned carefully. Penalties, in the form of excise taxes, are imposed (in most cases) if funds are withdrawn before the participant reaches age $59\frac{1}{2}$ (a 10% penalty), or if the participant fails to take minimum withdrawals by age $70\frac{1}{2}$ (a 50% penalty).

A NEGATIVE ELECTION 401(k) CAN BE A PLUS

If you run a company that sponsors a 401(k) plan, consider automatically enrolling all eligible employees. This may increase the amount that can be contributed by highly compensated employees, including yourself.

APRIL
15 **negative election 401(k)** a retirement plan design that calls for all eligible employees to participate in a 401(k) plan unless they expressly choose not to do so.

With a so-called *negative election 401(k)*, employees are deemed to have elected to defer a specified percentage of their pay (often 1% to 3%) unless they elect to defer a different amount, or nothing at all. Such a plan may make it easier for your company to pass nondiscrimination tests and thus permit top earners to boost their deferrals.

Boosting Your Benefits

To see how such a plan might work, suppose that you and a partner jointly own ABC Co. and earn $100,000 apiece. There are two other employees, both earning $10,000. You and your partner each wish to defer $7,500 (7.5% of pay) while the two employees defer $1,000 (10%) and zero, respectively.

	Compensation	*Desired Deferral*
You	$100,000	$7,500
Your partner	100,000	7,500
Manny	10,000	1,000
Moe	10,000	0

As you can see, the combined deferral for the rank and file equals 5% of pay ($1,000 out of $20,000). To pass a nondiscrimination test, the highly paids can't exceed that by more than two percentage points, so you and your partner would be limited to a 7% contribution, or $7,000 on a $100,000 salary: You could not contribute as much as you'd like.

Suppose you adopt a negative election 401(k) plan with an automatic 3% deferral. Assuming that the employee who did not participate goes along (many employees do) and that the other employee maintains a 10% deferral:

	Compensation	*Desired Deferral*
You	$100,000	$7,500
Your partner	100,000	7,500
Manny	10,000	1,000
Moe	10,000	300

Now, the total for the employee group increases from $1,000 (5% of $20,000) to $1,300 (6.5%). Thus, the upper limit for the highly paids increases to 8.5% (6.5% plus 2%) and you'll be able to make your desired 7.5% contribution.

From another perspective, the negative election permits you and your partner to raise your permitted deferral from 7% to 8.5% of pay.

RISK REDUCTION

What's the risk? You may have a fiduciary liability if employees don't specify how their contributions are to be invested. Sometime in the future you might wind up on the wrong end of a lawsuit, with employees charging that you were too conservative or too aggressive with their money.

To minimize this risk, consider depositing such automatic deferrals in a money market fund. Provide your employees with extensive information about investments. This gives them the opportunity and (presumably) the knowledge to direct their own investments, reducing your fiduciary liability.

There are other ways to increase participation among

employees: reducing the waiting period for eligibility and providing a company match. Nevertheless, a negative election plan may be an inexpensive, simple way to increase employee participation and thus raise your own 401(k) contributions.

BACK IN STYLE: DEFINED BENEFIT PLANS

Since the mid-1980s, defined benefit plans have gone out of favor, largely replaced by 401(k)s and various types of profit-sharing plans. However, some types of employers may be better off offering employees defined benefit plans.

As an employer, you may be a good candidate for a defined benefit plan if your company has the right demographics: You're in your late 40s or older with a younger staff that is not highly compensated and tends to turn over frequently. Over time, as lower-paid employees leave, contributions made on their behalf may be forfeited, which will reduce the ongoing costs of maintaining the plan.

A BREAK WITH TRADITION

Defined benefit plans are traditional pension plans, in which employers promise to pay retired employees a specific amount of income (the defined benefit), based on earnings and years of service. In order to fulfill this promise, large amounts of money must be put aside. If you are to receive a $100,000 annual pension, for example, your defined benefit plan might have to accumulate $1 million. Thus, your company may have to contribute hefty sums to the plan in order to reach that amount by the time you retire, and those contributions will be tax-deductible.

That was the reason defined benefit plans were so popular in prior years. A series of events, though, caused these plans to lose ground to 401(k)s and profit-sharing plans.

✔ The Tax Reform Act of 1986 reduced the maximum defined benefit from $145,000 per year to $90,000.

✔ New regulations changed the way in which contributions could be calculated, resulting in reduced contributions.

✔ The paperwork burden increased. With so many forms to fill out and so many nondiscrimination tests to pass, many employers decided not to spend the time and money necessary to sponsor a defined benefit plan.

✔ The stock market surge that began in mid-1982 had an effect, too. Many defined benefit plans performed better than actuaries had projected, so there was more money in these plans than expected. Employers were so far ahead of forecasted results that no further contributions could be made. From that point on, defined benefit plans didn't offer the advantages of wealth accumulation and tax shelter.

RELEGATING THE RESPONSIBILITY

Therefore, many employers turned to plans that shift the risk and the expense of retirement funding to employees. Contributions are not obligatory, as they are in defined benefit plans. Employees generally have been

---

Tax Tip Once an employer reaches age 48 or 50, the advantages of a defined benefit plan increase tremendously. A 45-year-old usually can contribute no more than $30,000 per year to a defined benefit plan, the same as the maximum that can go into a defined contribution account. By age 55, contributions as large as $80,000 are possible with a defined benefit plan, while the defined contribution limit remains at $30,000.

pleased because defined contribution plans allowed them to participate in the ongoing stock market boom.

Nevertheless, some employers may be better off with defined benefit plans. If there are older employers and younger employees, large amounts can be contributed on behalf of the business owners and relatively little for staff members.

TILTING THE SCALES

Suppose, for example, Mike Walker is a 55-year-old business owner earning $160,000 who employs a 28-year-old assistant earning $35,000. Each year, nearly $85,000 can be contributed to Mike's account while less than $4,000 is contributed for the assistant. If there is a five-year *vesting* requirement and the assistant leaves before five years, the plan retains all the money contributed for the assistant; this money (the assistant's *forfeitures*) can be used to reduce future mandated contributions to fund the plan.

What if the assistant stays for five years, to become vested? After five years, the present value of the assistant's future benefits will be less than $5,000 and the plan would be entitled to the rest of the assets, about $14,000 in this example. If the assistant stays until retirement age, the retirement benefit will equal 100% of annual salary, so these plans are an excellent way to reward loyal, longtime employees.

Ironically, legislative changes may now be favoring defined benefit plans. There is a provision in federal tax law called the "combined plan limit." If you have both a defined contribution plan and a defined benefit plan, you can get only 25% of the maximum benefit from a defined benefit plan. That rule expired after 1999, so participants will be able to maximize defined benefits as well as defined contributions. This change in the law may encourage employers who previously have terminated defined benefit plans to reinstate them, adding them to their defined contribution plans.

APRIL 15 **vesting**
the process in which employees must work for a company for a certain length of time before they're eligible to receive retirement benefits.

APRIL 15 **forfeitures**
funds in a retirement plan that are distributed among remaining participants when others leave before becoming fully vested.

PLUS AND MINUS

What about all of the disadvantages of defined benefit plans, as listed earlier? The annual defined benefit limit, set at $90,000 in the 1986 law, was indexed to inflation. By 2000, it had risen to $135,000 while the defined contribution limit was still $30,000 per year. (That $30,000 limit will remain effective until the defined benefit limit rises to $140,000, probably around 2002, at which time the defined contribution limit will be set at $35,000.)

Defined benefit plans still have drawbacks, notably contribution requirements and administration expenses.

The annual commitment may be a major concern. Employers may worry about having to make a large contribution if they have a bad year. In such circumstances, though, employers can amend the plan, reducing the benefit level. Holding down compensation in a poor year will also hold down the expected contribution.

As for expenses, a defined benefit plan may be less expensive than defined contribution plans in some situations. If a plan's investments yield more than the annual assumption, the excess may be used to reduce the required employer contribution. In addition, because defined benefit plans are not subject to 401(k) discrimination tests, they're often easier to administer.

401(k) FAULTS

With a 401(k) plan, the maximum pretax contribution in 2000 is $10,500, which may not be a meaningful amount to an employer trying to build a personal retirement fund. Moreover, a certain percentage of all employees must contribute to a 401(k).

If employees don't contribute sufficient amounts, employers may have to make 401(k) contributions for lower-compensated employees or reduce the amount that highly compensated employees may contribute. In some cases, owner-employees may not be allowed to contribute even the $10,500 maximum.

FOR LATE STARTERS

The bottom line is that it's difficult for, say, a 50-year-old who hasn't started saving for retirement to build up a substantial fund with a defined contribution plan, at $30,000 per year. With a defined benefit plan it can be done, especially if the plan includes a provision that allows a participant to catch up for past years of service to the company.

The key to a defined benefit plan is confidence in future income. Therefore, if you're a 50+ business owner with a predictable income stream from your company you may be willing to take on the obligations of a defined benefit plan, trusting in your ability to earn enough today that you'll be able to provide yourself a plump pension tomorrow.

CASH BALANCE PLANS MAY OFFER THE BEST OF BOTH WORLDS

cash balance plan a retirement plan that's actually a defined benefit (pension) plan but resembles a 401(k) plan to increase appeal to employees.

In recent years, many of America's top corporations have switched their pension plans to *cash balance plans*. Now, small companies are catching on to this strategy.

Cash balance plans are defined benefit plans, so they're particularly appealing to older business owners with a young, low-paid, high-turnover work force. As mentioned earlier, defined benefit plans can make very large contributions to the accounts of executives over age 50 while younger participants get little.

Rank-and-File Favorite

The skewing of benefits in a defined benefit plan may be a problem for company morale, though. Employee recruiting and retention may suffer. Cash balance plans, on the other hand, appeal to employees, too. Here's how they work:

1. Each participant gets an account that looks like the account in a 401(k) plan.

2. Workers receive annual contributions to these accounts, and those contributions may be based on age or years of service. Thus, your young employees may get a contribution that's a much smaller percentage of compensation than you receive.

3. The amounts in workers' accounts will grow regularly at some preset rate. The norm is 5%. (Although this increase looks like an investment return it really is not: The buildup is unrelated to the actual earnings of the money in the plan.)

4. Workers can check on their individual accounts so they'll see that they have something saved for their retirement. For many employees—especially younger ones—that's better than the promise of a payout from a defined benefit plan, sometime in the future.

5. Another attractive feature is that cash balances are portable, so workers can take their accounts when they leave. Young employees with no thought of staying around long enough to qualify for a pension will appreciate portability.

Moreover, you can set a five-year vesting requirement to shut out short-timers. Money that's forfeited stays in the plan, to reduce the amount that will have to be contributed in future years.

6. Similarly, if the plan earns more than the posted rate (which might be 5%), the excess will reduce required employer contributions in the future.

Something for Everyone

Therefore, cash balance plans may be extremely attractive. They offer generous benefits to older employers with younger workers. What's more, they avoid the expensive 401(k) discrimination tests so they may be cheaper to administer.

A cash balance plan may be particularly appealing if your company set up a defined benefit plan a few years ago that has grown into an *overfunded plan* because of strong stock market gains.

overfunded plan
a defined benefit plan that currently holds assets greater than those needed to make the required payments. At this point, further contributions are not permitted.

Simply terminating such a plan would generate a 50% excise tax as well as income tax consequences. Terminating a plan also requires immediate vesting for all participants and filing various government forms.

Instead, an overfunded defined benefit plan can be rolled over to a cash balance plan with no penalties, no vesting, and a smaller paperwork burden. Excess assets can be used for future funding of participants' benefits.

While you and your company are enjoying these financial benefits, cash balance plans may help you to attract and retain capable employees.

First Things First

So what's the catch with a cash balance plan? Defined benefit plans can be expensive to administer and cash balance plans are no exception. (Generally, the extra benefits will outweigh the extra costs, provided you're older than your employees.)

Moreover, cash balance plans work against older employees—including yourself—if the contribution is a flat percentage of pay for everyone. You need to work with an employee benefits professional who can come up with a plan design that will direct more money into your account.

SIMPLE SOLUTIONS

As indicated, 401(k)s, defined benefit plans, and cash balance plans all involve some expensive administration. You may prefer a plan with a minimum of paperwork and administrative expense.

The uncomplicated retirement plans that work best for self-employed individuals may not be the ideal choices for small companies. Here are some guidelines to help you choose.

FOR THE SELF-EMPLOYED, SELECT A SEP

If you're self-employed, a simplified employee pension (SEP) plan likely is the top choice. The benefits:

✔ *Paltry paperwork.* After you fill out a one-page form to set up the plan there are no further reports or annual tax filings.

✔ *Flexibility.* You can minimize or even omit your SEP contribution in a year when cash flow is meager.

✔ *Retroactive deductions.* Contributions to a SEP can be made anytime until the due date of your tax return, including extensions. For example, you can make a contribution to a new or existing SEP on April 15, 2001, and take a full deduction from your year 2000 taxable income.

If you want to make a tax-deductible contribution for the prior year and you have not already established a retirement plan, a SEP is your only choice.

✔ *Generous contribution limits.* The maximum you can contribute to a SEP each year is now $25,500 (15% of $170,000 in income). That $170,000 income limit will increase with inflation over the years so the maximum SEP contribution (and tax deduction) will increase, too.

Convoluted Calculations

The aforementioned 15% limit is 15% of your self-employment income after the SEP contribution. (You also must deduct one-half of your self-employment tax.)

The end result is that you actually can contribute less than 13% of gross self-employment income to a SEP. Thus, you'd need about $203,000 in self-employment income to make a maximum $25,500 SEP contribution.

Moreover, if your self-employment income is high enough (over $157,000) you can increase your contribution to $30,000 by adding a money purchase defined contribution plan to your SEP. However, you'll also add a paperwork burden and an obligation to make certain contributions each year.

Words to the Wise

SEPs are sometimes known as SEP-IRAs, but don't be confused. Even if you have a SEP you still can contribute up

Tax Tip On a complexity scale of 1 to 10, SEPs rate a 1 while qualified retirement plans such as money purchase plans rate a 10. Make sure the additional annual contribution you'll be allowed is worth the responsibility you'll assume.

to $2,000 per year to an IRA. If you meet certain income tests you can deduct that IRA contribution or contribute to a Roth IRA. Also, SEP accounts and IRA accounts can be combined.

SIMPLE PLANS FOR SMALL SUMS

If your self-employment income is less than $46,000, you'll be able to contribute less than $6,000 per year to a SEP: 13% of $46,000 is $5,980. In that case, you're better off with a SIMPLE (savings incentive match plan for employees) IRA.

You can contribute 100% of your self-employment income, up to $6,000. Suppose, for example, you have a day job and you also earn $10,000 this year as a consultant. You can contribute $6,000 (60%) of your consulting income to a SIMPLE IRA. With a SEP, your maximum contribution would be around $1,300 (13%).

SIMPLE plans permit a 3% match, so you could add another $300 if you have $10,000 in self-employment income.

Tax Tip SIMPLE 401(k) plans also are available but they're generally unappealing due to their relative complexity and administrative demands.

Although these plans may be slightly more complex than a SEP, they're still low-maintenance, perhaps 2 on that 1-to-10 scale.

THE BEST FOR BUSINESS OWNERS

As mentioned, SEPs are excellent plans for the self-employed. However, they're usually not desirable for companies with more than a few employees.

Why not? With a SEP, the employer is responsible for all contributions. If you contribute 15% of pay to your own account, you'll also have to contribute 15% of pay for your employees.

Today, most employers prefer to sponsor retirement plans that rely on employee contributions. What works for small companies?

SIMPLE IRAs ARE SUPERIOR

SIMPLE IRAs, previously described, are often the top choice for companies with up to 100 employees. In a company setting, the employer match can be as much as $6,000, bringing the total for your own account up to $12,000.

> **Tax Tip** Your spouse, children, and other relatives can have SIMPLE IRAs, too. As long as they legitimately earn at least $6,000 per year, they each can put $6,000 into a tax-deferred SIMPLE IRA, plus a 3%-of-compensation company match.

What's more, you and your relatives can maximize the tax benefits of SIMPLE IRAs even if none of your other employees contribute and no further company match is required.

In many cases, at least 70% of the money contributed will go to you and your relatives, with a SIMPLE IRA.

SECOND CHOICE: A SAFE HARBOR 401(k)

Safe harbor 401(k) plans, introduced in 1999, already are gaining popularity. They work the same as traditional 401(k)s, allowing employees to contribute up to $10,500 worth of compensation per year on a tax-deferred basis.

However, regular 401(k) plans have to pass nondiscrimination tests. Rank-and-file workers have to contribute certain amounts in order for highly compensated employees to maximize contributions.

With a safe harbor 401(k) you can enjoy an exemption from these nondiscrimination tests. What's required?

As an employer you must agree to a fully vested 100% match, up to 4% of compensation, or a 3% across-the-board match for all eligible employees.

Thus, if you're a highly compensated owner-employee, you can have up to $17,300 contributed to your account each year: a $10,500 salary deferral and a $6,800 (4% of $170,000) employer match. That's true regardless of whether other workers participate.

THINKING ABOUT A TRADITIONAL 401(k)?

With a regular 401(k) plan, no employer match is required. Thus, if you think that your work force will participate without any match and that you'll pass a nondiscrimination test, these plans may save you money. Without an employer match, though, your own account is limited to $10,500 per year.

Traditional 401(k)s may work in companies with high employee turnover because a seven-year vesting schedule is permitted. Otherwise, you may be better off with a SIMPLE IRA or a safe harbor 401(k).

What if you'd like to contribute more than $17,300 to your personal account, the amount permitted by a safe harbor 401(k)? Assuming that you're older than your employees, consider a defined benefit plan or a cash balance plan, as explained earlier in this chapter.

ALL HANDS ON THE WHEEL

In most of the retirement plans described so far, a certain amount is contributed on behalf of participants. In some cases, those contributions go into a pool that needs to be invested.

Thus, it's up to you, as plan sponsor, to make the investment decisions. You may hire a financial professional to help you decide.

In some cases, though, a company will have two or more co-owners—and these key players may not agree on how the money should be invested.

Suppose, for example, your company has four principals, ages 35 to 60. Because of this vast age disparity you each have radically different goals and risk tolerances. Therefore, all four owners want to control their own retirement funds.

In this situation, you can set up a *self-directed plan* with segregated accounts. Then everyone goes his or her own way.

Each of your company's principals can have an individual account, using different investment managers if desired.

Flexibility, at a Cost

There's a great deal of adaptability in this self-directed approach. You can invest solely in growth stocks, if that's your preference, and your partner can invest in Treasury bills.

This kind of flexibility will cost your company a bit more, but the extra expense involved in setting up the plan correctly likely will pay dividends over the life of the plan.

self-directed plans company-sponsored retirement plans that let employees make their own investment decisions with their personal accounts.

Previously, self-directed plans were extremely expensive because they needed specially drafted legal documents and complex accounting procedures. Now, *prototype plans* offered by some independent trust companies can be very cost-effective.

If you work with a savvy financial adviser, you can locate an independent trust company that charges $100 to $250 to provide a prototype self-directed plan. Such a trust company will also handle all of the annual accounting requirements such a plan generates for an additional $250 to $500 per year.

Banks, brokers, mutual fund companies, and insurers may also provide such plans.

> **prototype plans**
> easy-to-use retirement plans provided to employers by trust companies, brokers, mutual fund companies, and insurers.

Including Your Employees

If you and your partners each have a personalized account for investing retirement plan contributions, what happens to contributions for the benefit of your employees? They'll have separate accounts, too.

A financial adviser might meet with your employees and guide them to proper investment choices. In fact, it's in your interest to retain such a professional.

Offloading the Responsibility

Why should you pay an investment adviser to counsel your workers? Because you could wind up facing lawsuits if your employees' plans provide low returns. On the other hand, if you make reasonable efforts to see that your employees are well advised they are likely to prosper while you'll reduce your own liability.

Make sure that adviser meets regularly with each participant or conducts periodic employee information meetings. Several investment choices should available, not just proprietary products sponsored by one brokerage firm, bank, or insurance company.

In addition, you should keep records of all your efforts to educate participants. You can't force an employee to make good decisions, but you can show that you made good investment choices available and made a diligent effort to communicate those choices to your employees.

PLAYING BY THE PRUDENT PERSON RULES

If you're the owner of a company that sponsors a retirement plan, you have *fiduciary responsibility*. Thus, you must invest "prudently."

> **fiduciary responsibility** the obligation of a retirement plan sponsor or trustee to invest plan money wisely on behalf of all participants.

That is, you must comply with complex rules established by the IRS and the Department of Labor. Money in a retirement plan is not your money any longer; you're not allowed to use that money for personal or business purposes.

Impact: Imprudence will likely draw penalties from the regulators, while plan participants may sue you for poor handling of trust assets.

The Greater Good

Under the so-called *prudent investor guidelines*, fiduciaries must look at the entire portfolio, taking appropriate risks in search of suitable awards. Therefore, proven stocks and high-grade bonds should be the foundation of your retirement plan.

> **prudent investor guidelines** requirements that a fiduciary must invest with the entire portfolio in mind, taking reasonable risks in order to achieve substantial returns.

You might include some real estate, too, although you'll have to cope with valuation and liquidity issues. You can speculate with perhaps 10% of the portfolio, as long as you document a decent chance your long shot will pay off.

SHUN SUPER-SAFETY

Investing all of a fund's money in Treasuries or certificates of deposit (CDs) won't keep you out of trouble. Such vehicles have underperformed equities in virtually every extended time period. If your plan earns, say, 5% per year in low-risk investments while the major stock market averages go up 20% per year, you may have to pay all or part of the differential (which could be considerable) to employees.

You should, however, hold some money in T-bills or money market funds that can quickly be converted to cash without risk of loss. The older your employee group, and the closer your obligation to pay distributions, the greater your need for ready cash.

GO WITH A PRO

If you're running your own business, you may not want to spend a lot of time running the retirement plan's investment portfolio. You can hire a professional adviser but, if you do, you should lay an adequate paper trail.

1. Get the names of several potential advisers. Each should be a qualified professional, with designations such as certified financial planner, chartered financial consultant, or personal financial specialist.

2. Interview each candidate. Take notes on your interview and check references.

3. When you make a decision, enter the reasons into your corporate minutes. Your adviser should be an unrelated party, with no conflicts of interest.

4. Sign a letter of engagement with your adviser. All compensation should be disclosed. The adviser should also prepare a formal investment policy statement for your retirement plan, spelling out your objectives and the means that will be used to meet them.

5. Monitor your adviser's progress with regular meetings (at least once a year). Issue reports to all participants.

6. If your adviser is not performing as promised, start looking for a new adviser.

More Upside, Less Downside

This may seem like a convoluted process—and it is. So why bother?

✔ Working with a skilled professional can help you build wealth inside your retirement plan, for yourself and your employees. The S&P 500 gained over 20% per year from 1991 through 1999; did your plan perform anywhere near as well?

✔ A savvy pro can help you avoid the types of *prohibited transactions* that can draw severe IRS and Labor Department penalties. You're not supposed to sell property to your own plan, for example, even at a fair price.

prohibited transactions investment activities forbidden to fiduciaries.

✔ All this paperwork can protect you against a suit by an unhappy employee. Suppose, for example, you decided to invest in Japanese stocks in 1989, right before the Japanese market tanked. You'd be in a much stronger position, in any litigation, if you can show you made what seemed like a reasonable decision at the time, based on expert advice.

Chapter

Investing for the
Truly Long Term

 fter you retire (or if you change jobs), you'll have to decide what to do with the money in your retirement plan. Here are your options:

✔ Withdraw the money.
✔ Take an annuity.
✔ Roll the money into a new retirement plan.
✔ Roll the money into an IRA.
✔ Roll to an IRA, then convert to a Roth IRA.

Each option has its pros and cons. If you know them beforehand, you'll be able to make the best choice.

WITHDRAWAL GAINS

Many retirement plans offer you the chance to receive your balance in a lump sum. You'll get your hands on your money but you'll immediately owe income tax on the money you receive, plus a 10% penalty tax if you're not yet $59\frac{1}{2}$.

> **APRIL**
> **15**
>
> **Tax Tip**   You'll be able to use 10-year averaging to reduce the tax bite if you were born before 1936.

(Five-year averaging was previously available, but that tax break expired after 1999.)

Ten-year averaging does not permit you to spread out your tax payments; you'll recognize taxable income in the year you receive the money. However, you will pay tax at lower rates.

The way the math works, 10-year averaging is truly effective only for distributions under $100,000. Therefore, you might want to put a small retirement plan balance into your pocket, if you qualify for 10-year averaging.

Otherwise, the only reason to cash in your retirement plan is if you have a desperate need for ready cash.

LIFELONG CASH FLOW FROM AN ANNUITY

Some retirement plans offer to convert your account balance into an income stream, especially when you retire. You'll usually receive such payments each month for your lifetime or for the lives of yourself and your spouse. In most cases, such annuity payments will be taxable.

The big advantage to receiving an annuity is security. You know that your retirement income will never stop.

However, some employers pay relatively low annuities to their retirees. If receiving an annuity appeals to you, you may be better off rolling your plan balance into an IRA, as explained next. Then you can use the money in your IRA to buy the most attractive annuity, after shopping among insurance companies.

FROM THE OLD TO THE NEW

If you're changing jobs, you may be able to roll your money from your old employer's to your new employer's retirement plan. Such a rollover maintains the tax deferral.

This option may be appealing if you don't want to manage your own investments. Your new employer's plan might be managed by a knowledgeable professional, relieving you of that responsibility.

Inside your new employer's plan, your account balance will continue to be protected from creditors. If you need cash, you may be able to borrow a certain amount, tax-free, with little hassle.

On the other hand, you won't have control of your money if you roll your retirement plan balance into your new employer's plan. You'll likely face restrictions on the access you'll have to this money.

Therefore, the attractiveness of this option will depend on specific circumstances. If your new employer has an outstanding retirement plan, consider a rollover.

REWARDING IRA ROLLOVERS

If you want to control your own finances, an IRA rollover likely will be the best choice. You can invest virtually any way that you'd like while your tax deferral is maintained.

Such rollovers:

✔ Must occur within 60 days of the distribution, and

✔ Must be transferred directly from trustee to trustee to avoid any adverse tax consequences.

Generally, your IRA will be funded with cash, which you'll be responsible for investing, rather than securities from your previous plan.

Remember that partial IRA rollovers provide the same advantages. Suppose, for example, you retire with $300,000 in your plan and you need $80,000 to clean up your credit card debt and to make a down payment on a mountain cabin. You could roll over $180,000 to an IRA while taking the remaining $120,000 in cash. On that $120,000, you'll owe income tax and possibly a 10% early withdrawal penalty, leaving you with enough for your cash needs.

In many cases, an IRA rollover or a partial rollover will be your best choice. However, don't implement a rollover without being aware of these disadvantages:

✔ In some states, IRAs don't enjoy the same creditor protection as an employer-sponsored plan.

✔ You can't borrow from an IRA.

✔ Money that has been rolled into an IRA is not eligible for 10-year averaging.

If you're married, you'll probably need your spouse's written acceptance of your choice. Without such consent, a rollover may be invalidated and the entire amount might become taxable income.

ROTH IRAs II: CONVERSIONS

In Chapter 7 the Roth IRA was described. As mentioned, contributions up to $2,000 per year are generally allowed.

What's more, you can convert a regular IRA (including a large rollover IRA) to a Roth IRA. You'll have to pay the deferred income tax, but, after converting, if you hold on to a Roth IRA at least five years until you're older than $59\frac{1}{2}$, you'll owe no tax on the withdrawals.

Exception: If you are married, filing separately, you are ineligible to convert an existing IRA to a Roth IRA.

A *Roth IRA conversion* is permitted only if your adjusted gross income does not exceed $100,000 on a single or joint return. (The income you realize from the conversion itself won't count toward this limit.)

There are no required withdrawals from a Roth IRA, so you can maintain the tax-free buildup throughout your lifetime, if desired.

A Roth IRA conversion probably will make sense if you expect to let the money grow for at least 10 years before any withdrawals. Such conversions work best if you can pay the up-front tax with non-IRA money, keeping the Roth IRA intact.

Roth IRA conversion
change of a regular IRA to a Roth IRA, which triggers an obligation to pay the deferred income tax.

PENALTY BOX

Anyone who takes money out of an IRA or other tax-deferred retirement plan will owe income tax, assuming the plan has been funded with deductible contributions. In addition, a 10% penalty tax is generally due on withdrawals before age $59^1/_2$. Taking out $5,000, for example, would mean a $500 penalty tax. Fortunately, there are several exceptions to the early withdrawal penalty:

✔ *Broad exceptions.* These exceptions apply to withdrawals from all tax-deferred retirement plans, including 401(k)s and IRAs:

Death. If someone dies and names you as the beneficiary of a retirement plan, you can withdraw the funds and avoid the 10% penalty, no matter what your age.

Disability. If you can't work, the 10% penalty won't be assessed.

Substantially equal periodic payments (SEPPs). To avoid the penalty, SEPPs must be based on your life expectancy. Once started, they must continue for at least five years, past age $59^1/_2$, or whichever comes later.

Medical expenses. The 10% penalty will be waived in the case of money withdrawn up to the amount of deductible medical expenses.

Suppose you have adjusted gross income (AGI) of $60,000 in 1999 and medical expenses of $12,000. Deductible medical expenses start at 7.5% of AGI, or $4,500 in your case. Thus, you would be $7,500 over the threshold so you could withdraw $7,500 from your retirement plan, penalty-free.

AGI	$60,000
Medical expenses	12,000
Threshold for deducting medical expenses (7.5% times $60,000)	(4,500)

substantially equal periodic payments (SEPPs) withdrawals from a tax-deferred retirement plan based on life expectancy. If these payments last at least five years and past age $59^1/_2$, there will be no 10% penalty for early withdrawals.

Deductible amount ($12,000 minus
$4,500)   7,500

Penalty-free retirement plan withdrawal $7,500

✔ *Qualified plan exceptions.* These exceptions apply only to withdrawals from employer-sponsored plans:

Separation from service. If you retire or change jobs, you can withdraw money, penalty-free, if the separation occurs during or after the year you reach age 55.

Qualified domestic relations orders (QDROs). In a divorce or marital separation, a QDRO is an order to the qualified plan's administrator to transfer part of one spouse's interest in the plan to the other spouse. The 10% tax on withdrawals before age 59$\frac{1}{2}$ does not apply to payments made to a spouse or ex-spouse under a QDRO.

✔ *IRA exceptions.* The separation-from-service and QDRO exceptions don't apply to early distributions from IRAs. However, there are some IRA-only loopholes:

Higher education. Distributions from IRAs to pay post–high school expenses are exempt from the 10% penalty. Eligible expenses include tuition, room and board, fees, books, supplies, and required equipment. Qualifying expenses can be yours, your spouse's, your children's, even your grandchildren's.

Health insurance. If you are out of work for at least 12 consecutive weeks you can take enough money from an IRA to keep your health insurance in force, penalty-free, and keep doing so until you're back to work for 60 days.

First home purchase. You also may take penalty-free withdrawals up to $10,000 for a first-time home purchase. To qualify, you cannot have had an ownership interest in a residence during the previous two years.

As you can see, some of these exceptions (death, disability, divorce) are available only in certain unfortunate circumstances. However, there is one technique that most people can use: the exception for SEPPs. All IRA owners can use the SEPP exception at any time, while participants in other plans can use SEPPs after separation from service.

What's more, the SEPP rules can be massaged so that you can take out virtually any amount you need, penalty-free. If you need to take money from a retirement plan before age 59$^1/_2$, calculate the amount that you'll need, after tax, for living expenses.

Once you have a number for your desired stream of withdrawals, contact the bank, brokerage firm, or mutual fund company that acts as the plan custodian. The custodian will make the necessary calculations and determine the method you should use to arrive at the chosen amount.

If you decide to receive SEPPs, keep in mind the five-year, age 59$^1/_2$ requirement. If you don't maintain the SEPPs for five years or until age 59$^1/_2$, you'll owe the 10% penalty tax on all withdrawals, retroactively. Thus, once you get started it pays for you to stay the course.

FOR EARLY BIRDS

Early retirement can be a problem if you rely on income from a tax-deferred retirement plan. Before age 59$^1/_2$, you'll probably owe a 10% penalty tax as well as income tax on all withdrawals.

One strategy to avoid the penalty tax: Use some or all of your retirement plan to purchase an *immediate annuity*. With this option, you can start to receive regular income right away and the 10% penalty won't apply.

What's more, an immediate annuity provides a lifelong income stream, no matter how long you live. If you and your spouse are both 65, there is a 25% probability that one of you will live until age 95, so you may appreciate the long-term security.

Traditionally, immediate annuities have paid out fixed amounts with no adjustment for inflation. Moreover, they offered you no access to your money: One day you had a large sum in your retirement account, but after an-

immediate annuity
a contract in which you give money to an insurance company, bank, or such, and get back an income stream that starts right away.

nuitizing (choosing an immediate annuity) all you had was a monthly or quarterly check.

Today, many immediate annuities offer variable payouts, meaning your income can grow if the funds are invested wisely. In addition, you may have liquidity options:

✔ You might be able to withdraw 20% of your assets each year, even after annuitizing.

✔ You might be able to take out some or even all of your money in the first five years after annuitizing.

✔ You might have access to a sum of money in case of an emergency, such as a medical crisis.

Mutual fund companies and banks have begun to aggressively promote immediate annuities, competing with insurance companies. The more competition, the higher the payouts that will be available, if you shop around.

Just because you've built up a retirement fund with one bank or mutual fund company doesn't mean you have to buy its immediate annuity; you can transfer your funds to another company with a better deal on an immediate annuity, tax-free.

FROM RETIREMENT PLAN TO A FABULOUS LEGACY

required minimum distribution amount that must be withdrawn from a tax-deferred retirement plan after age 70$^{1}/_{2}$ upon pain of a 50% penalty tax.

While many investors look to their pension or IRA to fund their retirement, others have enough outside assets that they would rather maintain the maximum tax-deferred growth possible by withdrawing annually only the minimum allowable amount. This latter group of investors hopes eventually to pass sizable retirement plan assets to the next generation.

Unfortunately, this strategy can backfire without careful planning. At a plan owner's death, income tax and estate tax may be due. Together, these taxes can eat up more than 75% of IRA or pension assets, leaving less than 25% left for the children.

However, more favorable tax treatment is possible. If the IRA or pension owner is married, he or she can designate a spouse as the plan beneficiary and take the *required minimum distributions* (those distributions mandatory after age 70$^1/_2$) over a joint life expectancy. With a joint life expectancy, required distributions are reduced because it is anticipated that payments will continue over a longer period of time. Thus, smaller required distributions allow for greater tax deferral on the remaining principal.

SPOUSAL STRATEGIES

An IRA owner or pension plan participant can leave retirement assets to a surviving spouse. The benefits from this decision are twofold.

First, use of the unlimited marital tax deduction (discussed in Chapter 13) probably will eliminate federal estate tax on such assets at the time of the participant's death.

Second, the surviving spouse typically can roll these funds over into an IRA, treating the balance as if it were his or her own. The surviving spouse not only will enjoy the benefit of further tax deferral, but also may be able to choose a minimum distribution schedule based on a joint life expectancy with a newly named beneficiary. (See Figure 9.1.)

Thus, in this example, the widow Barbara Smith names her son Bill as IRA beneficiary and begins to stretch distributions over a 23.5-year life expectancy.

SETTING UP A "SUPER-IRA"

Another potential alternative may be to name children or grandchildren as *designated beneficiaries* of retirement assets. While distributions during the IRA owner's lifetime (based on a joint-life distribution schedule) must be calculated on the premise that the beneficiary is no more than 10 years younger than the owner, once the owner dies it may be possible for the beneficiary to take distributions based on his or her own actual life expectancy.

If that beneficiary is very young, payments will be small, allowing for tremendous, continuing tax deferral over the beneficiary's lifetime. (Naming a grandchild may

**designated
beneficiaries**
individuals or
certain trusts
named to inherit
a retirement
account.

FIGURE 9.1   Example of a Spousal Rollover

In 2000, Bob Smith and his wife, Barbara, are ages 69 and 68, respectively. In 2000, Bob and Barbara's joint life expectancy is 21.9 years. Bob dies in year 2004 at age 73. Barbara then establishes a spousal rollover and names their 44-year-old son, Bill, as beneficiary. Barbara, age 73 in 2005, continues to take required distributions.

Year	Age	Life Expectancy	Government's Life Expectancy	Actual Joint Life Expectancy
2000	69	21.9		
2001	70	20.9		
2002	71	19.9		
2003	72	18.9		
2004	73	17.9		
2005	73[1]	16.9	23.5[2]	39
2006	74	15.9	22.7	
2007	75	14.9	21.8	
2008	76	13.9	20.9	
2009	77	12.9	20.1	
2010	78	11.9	19.2	
2011	79	10.9	18.4	
2012	80	9.9	17.6	
2013	81	8.9	16.8	
2014		7.9		30[3]
2015		6.9		29
2016		5.9		28
2017		4.9		27
2018		3.9		26
2019		2.9		25
2020		1.9		24
2021		.9		23

[1] In 2005, Barbara is 73. She establishes a spousal rollover and names 44-year-old Bill as beneficiary.
[2] While Barbara's actual joint life expectancy with Bill is 39, because of the incidental death benefit Bill is considered only 10 years younger than Barbara. Therefore, for purposes of calculating minimum distributions, their joint life expectancy is only 23.5 years.
[3] When Barbara dies at age 81, Bill will use their actual joint life expectancy for the remaining required distributions.

lead to generation-skipping transfer tax consequences, discussed in Chapter 13.)

Yet another strategy involves leaving retirement plan benefits to charity, through vehicles such as the private foundation or charitable remainder trust (discussed in Chapter 13). If the plan owner is married, the surviving spouse might consider leaving retirement plan assets to charity.

A thoughtful integration of both tax and philanthropic considerations can result in enhanced income for the plan owner's heirs as well as a substantial charitable contribution.

CHARITABLE THOUGHTS

If you have both an IRA (or another tax-deferred retirement account) and charitable intentions, name the charity as beneficiary of your retirement plan. At the same time, hold on to appreciated assets so you can leave them to your heirs with a basis step-up.

Suppose, for example, you're unmarried (widowed or divorced) with a total estate of $1 million. Half of that is in an IRA and the other half is in appreciated real estate and appreciated shares of your closely held company. You want to leave $500,000 to your children and $500,000 to your favorite charity. Making a $500,000 charitable gift will bring your estate below the $650,000 threshold so no estate tax will be due.

Income taxes, though, are another story. If the appreciated assets are left to charity while the IRA goes to your kids, your heirs eventually will have to pay income tax on all the money as it comes out of the IRA. If you assume a 40% income tax rate, your heirs will actually inherit $300,000, not $500,000. State and local income taxes might further reduce their inheritance.

Instead, suppose you leave your IRA to charity and bequeath the appreciated assets to your children. Again, there will be no estate tax but your children will inherit the appreciated assets with a step-up in basis. If they decide to sell those assets, they won't owe any capital gains tax on appreciation during your lifetime. They'll inherit a full $500,000.

Therefore, this approach—IRA to charity and appreciated assets to loved ones—can pass on such an estate completely tax-free and save hundreds of thousands of dollars in taxes. (Larger estates may owe estate tax.)

PUTTING YOUR SPOUSE FIRST

If you decide that this strategy makes sense, there are still some choices that need to be made. Should you leave your IRA directly to a charity or charities? Generally, outright bequests make sense if you are not married or if the bequest is relatively small in relation to the entire estate. Otherwise, your surviving spouse won't want to give up the IRA. (State law may require spousal consent.)

If you're married, then, you may prefer to leave your IRA money to your spouse, who in turn can leave the IRA to charity. This approach, though, assumes that your surviving spouse will be able to handle the IRA wisely, despite advancing age, and will ultimately make the appropriate charitable bequest.

Some surviving spouses will be able to follow this course but others will benefit from some control or protection. In these cases, a trust may be preferred.

With some trusts, all payouts from the IRA go to the surviving spouse. In case of need, the trustee can distribute more funds to the survivor. At the second death, the money left in the IRA goes to the charity named by the first spouse to die, and no tax is due.

This sort of arrangement provides outstanding flexibility (providing a reliable trustee is named) but there's always the chance that the surviving spouse will live so long that all the IRA money will be paid out, leaving nothing to charity.

An alternative, therefore, is for you to leave your IRA to a charitable remainder trust (CRT) and name your spouse as "income beneficiary." You can limit your spouse's income to, say, 8% of trust assets per year, assuring that there will be a trust fund to eventually pass to charity.

KEEP THE CASH FLOWING

Another factor must be considered when you are choosing among outright donations and various trusts for IRA bequests. Naming a charitable trust or a charity as beneficiary will reduce your ability to prolong IRA distributions while you're still alive.

Impact: A charitable trust or a charity has no life expectancy, so naming one as the beneficiary means using a single-life expectancy (yours) and speeding withdrawals.

On the other hand, with a "designated beneficiary" (a person) a joint life expectancy may be used. The same is true with certain types of trusts, if they have individual beneficiaries. Therefore, if you leave your IRA directly to your spouse or to certain types of trusts, you can use a joint life expectancy, stretching out minimum distributions and extending the tax-free buildup.

DIVIDE TO CONQUER

The strategies just described assume that you have $500,000 in an IRA and you want to leave $500,000 to charity. More likely, you might want to leave only $50,000 or $100,000 to charity. If that's true, you should avoid making a specific bequest from an IRA or qualified plan. If you specify a $50,000 bequest from a $500,000 IRA, the IRS will treat that as a $50,000 withdrawal from the IRA and assess income tax on the $50,000.

As an alternative, you might name cobeneficiaries, perhaps saying that 10% of the IRA goes to charity while 90% goes to a family member. However, in the case of multiple IRA beneficiaries, the one with the shortest life expectancy is used when calculating minimum withdrawals. Because a charity has no life expectancy, a single-life expectancy would have to be used, accelerating income taxes after required minimum distributions begin.

To avoid this problem yet still make a partial IRA bequest, split your IRA. With $500,000 in an IRA you could roll over $50,000 to a new IRA, tax-free. The charity could be named as beneficiary for the new $50,000 IRA while a family member remains the beneficiary for the old $450,000 IRA.

CLOSE CALLS

When you split your IRAs in this manner you need to monitor them closely. Suppose you split off a $50,000 IRA at age 60. Assuming a 9% growth rate, that IRA will hold $100,000 at age 68, $200,000 at age 76. Do you really want to leave $200,000 to one charity? Further IRA splitting may be necessary.

If you split your IRAs and follow them closely, overall estate planning may be advanced. Suppose you divide a $550,000 IRA into a $250,000 IRA with your spouse as beneficiary, a $250,000 IRA with your daughter as beneficiary, and a $50,000 IRA with a charity as beneficiary. When you pass age $70^1/_2$ and minimum withdrawals must begin, the various life expectancies might dictate that you withdraw at least $25,000 in order to avoid a 50% penalty tax.

These amounts need not be withdrawn pro rata from each IRA; if a total of $25,000 is withdrawn, no penalty will be due. Assuming the charitable IRA earned $4,500, you might withdraw that $4,500 to keep the balance at $50,000. The other $20,500 might be drawn from the spousal IRA while your daughter's IRA remains intact. (If there's more than one child, IRAs can be split so that they each inherit one.)

The same strategy can be pursued each year, as long as you're alive. The charitable IRA will remain at the desired $50,000 level while the rest of the withdrawals come out of the spousal IRA, providing retirement income. Your daughter's IRA can continue to grow as long as it doesn't exceed the current estate tax threshold.

Assuming you're the first spouse to die, the charity will get its $50,000 IRA, your surviving spouse will inherit what's left of the spousal IRA (along with your other assets), while your daughter inherits a large IRA. Under current law you can leave your children up to $1 million (in total) and no estate tax will be due, assuming you die after 2005.

Your surviving spouse can draw down the rest of the IRA while still alive and leave appreciated assets to your daughter with a full step-up in basis. Your daughter, meanwhile, can stretch distributions from her IRA over several decades, extending the tax-deferred wealth building.

Such savvy IRA estate planning can provide for charity, for a surviving spouse, and for future generations, leaving as little as possible for the IRS.

LONG-LASTING LEGACY

To see how a multigenerational IRA might work, consider the circumstances of Mark Jones, a 70-year-old widower with a gross estate of $4 million and a $2 million IRA rollover from his former employer. Mark has named two adult children as beneficiaries.

If Mark was married and left the plan assets directly to his spouse, taxes would not apply until her death. Eventually, though, estate and income taxes could quickly erode the value of the plan assets passing to beneficiaries.

To create a multigenerational IRA, several important decisions must be made prior to the *required beginning date* of the plan participant. First, Mark must select a designated beneficiary and make life expectancy elections.

In most cases the designated beneficiary is a spouse, whose life expectancy can be used along with Mark's to measure the maximum withdrawal period over which distributions may be taken from the qualified plan. In the case of a plan participant who is single at the required beginning date, the children or an irrevocable trust may be substituted as a designated beneficiary.

required beginning date
the date when retirement plan withdrawals must begin, April 1 of the next year after you reach $70^{1}/_{2}$.

The second election that Mark must take, which becomes irrevocable as of the required beginning date, is the use of the recalculation or the nonrecalculation election period.

Under many qualified planning provisions, Mark would have the option to elect to recalculate either his life expectancy or that of his spouse, or both. Recalculation is only available if the designated beneficiary is the spouse

recalculation method

a method of withdrawing retirement plan money that extends the recipients' life expectancy each year.

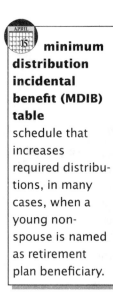

minimum distribution incidental benefit (MDIB) table

schedule that increases required distributions, in many cases, when a young non-spouse is named as retirement plan beneficiary.

of the plan participant. The *recalculation method* generally allows for a longer withdrawal period, as life expectancy does not decrease by one full year each calendar year. However, once the measuring life dies, recalculation accelerates distributions and all plan proceeds must be distributed in the year after the plan participant's death.

FROM A DECADE TO A DYNASTY

An excellent planning opportunity is available for a surviving spouse who elects to treat the deceased spouse's IRA rollover as his or her own or an individual who is single as of the required beginning date. Either prior to the required beginning date or on receipt of the spousal rollover, one solution would be to name the children or grandchildren as designated beneficiaries.

Under these circumstances, special tables called *minimum distribution incidental benefit (MDIB) tables* would measure distributions. These tables apply when a nonspouse beneficiary who is more than 10 years younger than the plan owner is the designated beneficiary. The MDIB tables assume that the designated beneficiary is always 10 years younger than the plan owner.

The most attractive feature about the MDIB tables is that they terminate the year after the surviving spouse or plan participant's death. At this point, the beneficiaries may take withdrawals over their remaining life expectancy as determined when the surviving spouse rolled over the IRA with a reduction for every year that has elapsed.

Allowing the children to take distributions over the remaining lifetime allows them to stretch income tax deferral well beyond the parent's lifetime. This benefit of extended tax deferral becomes even more valuable if grandchildren are named as designated beneficiaries.

Split Decision

In the event that there is more than one child or grandchild who will be named as the designated beneficiary, it may make sense on receipt of the IRA rollover or prior to the required beginning date to split the IRA into three separate rollover IRAs for each designated beneficiary. In this manner, the younger beneficiaries may extend the tax deferral longer than that of their older counterparts.

Ready Cash

A crucial element in any plan in which a multigenerational IRA is desired is the liquidity to pay applicable transfer taxes. When the plan participant or surviving spouse passes away, the value of the IRA account will be included in the estate subject to estate tax.

If qualified plan assets are liquidated to pay the transfer taxes, the purpose of the multigenerational IRA is somewhat defeated. Also, this liquidation will incur income taxes, indicated in the previous example. Estate liquidity may be created in several ways. The plan participant may systematically liquidate additional qualified plans and reinvest in nonqualified accounts within the estate.

Another, more efficient method of providing liquidity involves the use of a single-life or survivorship life insurance contract designed to be payable upon the death of the plan participant. If there is sufficient liquidity to offset transfer taxes upon the plan participant's death, beneficiaries may continue to enjoy the benefits of tax-deferred compounding over their lifetimes.

Favored Policy

Because of the leverage and the income tax–favored treatment afforded life insurance products, often they become a preferred alternative. Policies are typically owned by the participant's children or an irrevocable trust established for their benefit and are purchased through annual gifts from the plan participant.

If the trust established for this purpose contains dynasty provisions and includes grandchildren as beneficiaries, the plan may also create a multigenerational trust to complement the multigenerational IRA.

Rough Seas

Your IRA or other tax-deferred plan may well be the most valuable legacy you leave to your loved ones. However, many financial institutions are unwilling or unable to provide the necessary support.

As a result, in many cases, IRA withdrawals are accelerated, depriving beneficiaries of years of tax-deferred compounding. The shortfall may add up to hundreds of thousands—even millions—of dollars.

TEXTBOOK CASE

Ideally, an IRA stretch-out goes something like this:

1. You take minimum distributions, beginning after you reach age $70^1/_2$, based on your life expectancy and that of a named beneficiary, typically your spouse.

2. After your death, your spouse rolls over your IRA to the spouses's own, names new beneficiaries (such as your children), and begins a new schedule of minimum distributions.

3. After your spouse dies, the children continue the minimum distributions over their life expectancy, which might be 30 or 40 years or longer.

4. If your children die before reaching the end of the payout period, the distributions continue until the end of that period has been reached, payable to beneficiaries they have designated.

NO SPOUSE NECESSARY

The previous scenario assumes you have a spouse you wish to name as IRA beneficiary. If not, you can leave your IRA to your children or even your grandchildren and have them enjoy the stretch-out benefits.

For example, suppose Jean Jones dies at age 69 with $650,000 in her IRA, naming her 35-year-old son Jim as beneficiary. Assuming the IRA earns a modest 7% per year, Jim can pull out more than $1 million over the next 25 years and still have nearly $2 million in the account.

CONTRARY CUSTODIANS

Your heirs may not enjoy such good fortune, though, if your IRA custodian (typically a bank, a brokerage firm, or a mutual fund family) doesn't go along. Possible reasons:

✔ *Short stop.* Some IRA custodians won't let IRA beneficiaries name their own beneficiaries. At the first beneficiary's death, the IRA terminates. As a result, all the remaining assets are distributed, and income taxes are due.

For example, suppose Alice Adams dies and her IRA passes to her daughter Beth, who has a 35-year life expectancy at that point. Beth dies 25 years later. Some IRA custodians will let Beth's beneficiary, her daughter Carol, spread out distributions over 10 years. However, some won't allow the last 10 years of the stretch-out.

✔ *Faulty forms.* Many IRA providers' forms don't offer investors the opportunity to name multiple beneficiaries or successor beneficiaries.

✔ *Lost forms.* Some IRA providers will have lost the account's beneficiary forms. This is especially likely to happen when financial institutions have been merged.

Without a form, the IRA likely will be distributed to the IRA owner's estate. Then, the IRA must be paid within five years, if the owner had not begun minimum distributions. If minimum distributions had begun, the IRA may have to be paid out by December 31 of the year after the death.

A PROACTIVE APPROACH

How can you maximize long-term tax deferral?

When you establish an account with an IRA custodian, don't deal with the person sitting behind the customer service desk or with a phone rep. That person may have little or no training on complex IRA issues.

Insist on speaking with someone who's truly knowledgeable. Most institutions have senior people in the retirement department who keep up with such matters; be persistent until you find them.

Other pointers:

✔ Before placing your money with an IRA custodian, find out if it permits the *stretch-out IRA* you desire.

✔ Don't assume your tax preparer or family attorney knows all about IRAs and pensions. This is a complicated subject and keeping abreast is difficult. Hire a professional who's experienced in these matters.

✔ Don't use the beneficiary form provided by the IRA custodian. Some professionals have *customized beneficiary forms* you can send in.

✔ Whether you use the standard beneficiary form or a customized version, always submit duplicate copies. Ask for one copy to be acknowledged (stamped and dated) and returned. Keep your copy in a place that's accessible to the beneficiaries.

✔ If you already have one or more IRAs, make sure you have a form on file with the provider (that is, make sure it hasn't been lost). Ask the provider to send you an *acknowledged copy*.

✔ If your beneficiary form can't be located, fill out a new one or supply your own, using the procedures we've described.

✔ Check all the information on your beneficiary form for accuracy. Some errors—an incorrect birth date, for example—can have serious consequences.

✔ Ask your current IRA provider about its policy on stretch-out IRAs. If you're not happy, find a provider that will accommodate your plans.

✔ Don't name your estate as beneficiary or contingent beneficiary. To prevent a quick payout after your death, name one or more individuals or a qualified trust.

✔ Don't name a minor as beneficiary. Minors are not allowed to be IRA beneficiaries, so the issue may get tied up in court.

stretch-out IRA
an IRA that extends tax-free compounding to the children and perhaps even the grandchildren of the original owner.

customized beneficiary form
a form prepared by a professional adviser detailing how an inherited retirement account is to be distributed.

acknowledged copy
a signed and dated notice from a retirement plan custodian attesting to the receipt of a beneficiary designation.

✔ Make sure to specify a distribution method (recalculation, *term-certain method*, or *hybrid method*) by age 70$\frac{1}{2}$. If you don't make a choice, the IRA provider probably will use the recalculation method, even if that's not what you want. (If your IRA provider permits only the recalculation method, you may want to transfer your IRA.)

✔ Check closely on the minimum distribution calculations or have a professional adviser confirm the numbers. Mistakes, if not corrected, may be extremely costly over the long term.

BRIEFS FOR BENEFICIARIES

What if you inherit an IRA? Chances are that you'll need to act swiftly and surely to maximize your payout.

- ✔ Check that the beneficiary forms and related paperwork are in place.
- ✔ Find out if a long-term stretch-out will be permitted. If not, considering switching to a cooperative provider.
- ✔ Don't accept checks that terminate an inherited IRA if you want to maintain the tax-deferred compounding.
- ✔ Nonspouses should insist that the IRA provider keep the IRA in the deceased owner's name. If the IRA is retitled in the name of a nonspouse, distributions will be accelerated.
- ✔ If you need to move an IRA inherited from someone other than a spouse, use a direct transfer rather than taking possession of the money in the account.
- ✔ In case an IRA provider has lost or destroyed forms, consider legal action. IRA custodians are responsible for the related paperwork as well as for the assets in the account.

term-certain method
a retirement plan withdrawal method that fixes a time period.

hybrid method
a method that uses both the recalculation and term-certain method to provide both safety and extended tax deferral.

THE TRIPLE TAX PARLAY

The low-income housing tax credits described in Chapter 6 can mix nicely with required minimum distributions from an IRA or other retirement plan. This strategy is as follows:

Step One: Assume you have an existing qualified retirement plan, and you are over $59^1/_2$ years of age. It is important to keep in mind that the federal government may double-tax whatever plan assets you do not spend during your lifetime (or that of your spouse). After you (and your spouse) have died, the balance of your retirement plan will most likely be subject to a 75% to 80% transfer tax made up of income and estate taxes.

Thus, it makes sense to shrink qualified plan assets now, and convert them to estate-tax-protected assets. Yet, won't withdrawal of these qualified assets now trigger income tax? Not necessarily. The Triple Tax Parlay may allow you to withdraw up to $250,000 from your retirement plan, tax-free and asset-protected: (1) real estate tax credit, (2) tax-free gift to trust, and (3) insurance proceeds free of gift and estate tax.

Step Two: As explained in Chapter 6, most taxpayers have the opportunity to qualify for up to $25,000 in tax-free income, annually, through affordable housing tax credits.

✔ Assuming a 28% federal income tax bracket, a onetime, $58,000 tax credit investment can be made.

✔ Each year for approximately 10 years (subject to the initial start-up period of approximately 18 months while the housing is built and rented) you can receive up to a $7,000 tax credit.

✔ Coincidentally, $7,000 is the exact amount of federal income taxes owed on $25,000 of income withdrawn from your retirement plan.

At the end of the program, you will have been eligible to have withdrawn $250,000, free of income tax. Assuming the project general partners are able to sell the structures for at least as much as they cost, you will also likely receive your original $58,000 investment back. This $58,000 should be characterized as a return of capital, and should also be tax-free.

Step Three: Each year that you participate in the tax credit program, you can transfer the $25,000 of tax-free income withdrawn from your retirement plan into an irrevocable trust. You (and your spouse, if you're married) will be the trust creator. At the second spouse's death, the initial trust will subdivide into an individual trust for each of your children, offering them estate-tax-free and asset-protected funds. Whatever is not spent during each child's lifetime can be passed on to his or her children, your grandchildren, also estate-tax-free and protected from creditors.

Step Four: While an irrevocable trust can own almost any type of investment, such as stocks, bonds, CDs, and real estate, the most heavily tax-favored investment is *cash-rich life insurance* (see Chapter 11). Your annual income- and gift-tax-free contribution to the trust, when invested in cash-rich life insurance, can be multiplied into as much as $1 million for your family.

> **cash-rich life insurance** an insurance policy designed to build up a substantial investment account.

Furthermore, cash-rich life insurance is self-completing: If you do not live to complete the funding program, the policy will still pay out the full face value. Moreover, such insurance also avoids capital gains tax on the growth between the $250,000 of funding ($25,000 each year for 10 years) and the $1 million death benefit. Due to the special tax advantages offered this type of insurance by the government, the $750,000 gain is completely exempt from capital gains tax.

Chapter

Adding Annuities
to the Mix

From 1985 through the present, the federal government has implemented a barrage of new legislation intended to limit contributions to employer-sponsored retirement plans. Given the questionable viability of government retirement programs such as Social Security, the government's rationale for this legislative direction is unclear. What is clear, however, is that a taxpayer today cannot shelter nearly as much within a retirement plan as could an equally well-compensated peer several years ago.

For example, an executive who earned $235,840 annually and participated in a 30% defined benefit plan in 1993 could have had an annual projected pension distribution of $70,752 and could have contributed accordingly to such a plan. By 1999, however, that same individual earning $235,840 would have been limited to contributing as if earning only $160,000. Under that same 30% defined benefit plan, therefore, this executive's projected pension distribution would have been reduced to $48,000! That's a retirement shortfall of $22,752.

What does this mean for today's taxpayer? At retirement, your standard of living may suffer. Therefore, while qualified (employer-sponsored) pensions and IRAs are tremendous retirement planning tools, their increasingly

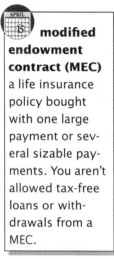

modified endowment contract (MEC) a life insurance policy bought with one large payment or several sizable payments. You aren't allowed tax-free loans or withdrawals from a MEC.

restrictive contribution limits make supplemental, non-qualified alternatives virtually imperative. Alternatives such as annuities and *modified endowment contracts (MECs)* are particularly attractive because they provide coveted tax deferral while offering greater flexibility than their qualified counterparts.

KEEP THE CASH FLOWING

Basically, an annuity is a contract between an investor and a financial institution such as an insurance company in which:

✔ The investor pays the company an agreed-upon sum of money.

✔ The company agrees to make regular payments to the investor.

✔ The payments may be for a lifetime or for a stated term.

✔ The payment obligation is determined by either the actual or the anticipated return on the initial investment.

POSTPONING THE PAYOFF

Both fixed and variable annuities allow the principal to grow on a tax-deferred basis. Further, when income is distributed, the principal and interest can be withdrawn on a tax-favored basis, known as annuitization.

Distributions are characterized partially as return of capital and partially as investment growth; only the growth portion is income taxable. Further, that taxation occurs at a time of your choosing because you are not taxed until you take withdrawals.

In sum, annuities have almost all of the advantages of an IRA, without the $2,000 annual contribution limit.

STOCK ANSWERS

Variable annuities offer multiple investment opportunities through various *subaccounts*, including some that resemble mutual funds. The return is tied to market performance; variable annuity investors are permitted cost-free switching of funds between subaccounts.

    Nonetheless, the most significant aspect of a variable annuity is its ability to make your earnings from mutual funds tax-deferred. While your money is accumulating, the dividends, interest, and capital gains that your portfolio(s) earn will not be subject to taxation at the federal or state level. Further, the annuity wrapper provides for an ever-increasing principal guarantee in the event of death.

    Many variable annuities offer a death benefit guaranteed to equal, at the very least, the value of the original investment.

 variable annuity
a deferred annuity that allows you to direct your investment into various accounts, including stock funds.

subaccounts
investment accounts inside a variable annuity, a variable MEC, or a variable life insurance policy.

> **Tax Tip** It makes sense to roll over a growing variable annuity every five to seven years in order to lock in those gains in the form of an increasing guaranteed death benefit. The increased account value will determine the new "original investment amount," which will become the new guaranteed death benefit minimum.

BETTER THAN A BANK

Typically, *fixed annuities* are similar to a CD in that they offer a fixed return. Thus, fixed annuities have the safety feature of predetermined income. (However, the interest rate can be reset periodically.)

    Often, consistent compounding at a conservative rate of return will meet, and even exceed, the return generated by speculative investment brilliance. The money you earn in a fixed annuity won't be subject to income tax

fixed annuity
a deferred annuity that promises to pay you an interest rate comparable to what you'd earn on a bond.

until you actually take it from the contract. What's more, annuity interest rates generally are higher than the yields on CDs and such, where you'll owe tax each year.

With a fixed annuity your account value goes up every year. There's no stock market risk. (There is some risk that the issuer will default, but investors have yet to lose money with fixed annuities.)

PAYING THE PENALTY

 **deferred annuity**
an investment in which you pay now, wait for many years, and then withdraw funds. Taxes on the investment buildup aren't due until the money is received.

Unfortunately, withdrawals from *deferred annuities* not only are subject to income tax, they're also subject to a 10% penalty tax until age 59$\frac{1}{2}$ (although penalties can be avoided if withdrawals are made on a systematic basis).

Nevertheless, the presence of the 10% early-withdrawal penalty means that these investments are most suitable if you're older than 59$\frac{1}{2}$ or certain you can wait until that age to tap the contract.

EXIT STRATEGIES

surrender charge
payment you owe to an annuity issuer if you withdraw too much, too soon.

Deferred annuities impose *surrender charges*, usually for at least the first six years of the contract. These penalties, which might be 6% or more, reduce your earnings from the contract. (Your principal is always 100% guaranteed by the issuer.)

Some fixed annuities offer you the chance to pull out monthly interest and 10% of your principal each year, free of surrender charges (but not free of income tax). Look for such features before buying.

BAIT AND SWITCH

So-called fixed annuities don't really offer fixed returns. Instead, an interest rate is set for a given time period, and then reset. As a result, you're at the mercy of the issuer.

In fact, many fixed annuities are sold on the basis of a high yield that's guaranteed for one year. Some insurers use first-year annuity rates as a come-on, then drop rates sharply. Bait-and-switch annuities may drop as low as 3% per year, while others pay higher yields.

What's more, if hefty surrender charges are in place, you may be locked in to a low-return contract.

AVOIDING THE SNARE

To keep from being ripped off in a fixed annuity, consider these tactics:

✔ Buy an annuity with a *bailout clause*. Such a provision permits you to withdraw your money from the contract without paying any surrender charges, if the reset yield drops below a certain level.

Of course, a bailout clause that's triggered when the yield is reset at 3% isn't very appealing. Look for a guaranteed 5% payout.

What will happen if you need to exercise a bailout clause? You can roll your principal into another annuity from any issuer, tax-free, under Section 1035 of the tax code.

✔ Buy from a reliable issuer. Ask what investors with 5- and 10-year-old fixed annuities are now receiving. If longtime investors are getting less than newcomers, you can expect similar treatment in the future.

✔ Buy an annuity where the surrender charges vanish after six years. Moreover, the surrender charges should gradually decline. For example, a 6% surrender charge might be in effect the first year, tapering off to 1% by the sixth year.

✔ Buy a fixed annuity with a rate that's guaranteed for as long as six years. If the surrender charges vanish by then, you can shop around for the best contract on the market after the initial guarantee period lapses.

✔ Divide your fixed-annuity money among two or more contracts. You might buy three fixed annuities:

bailout clause
an escape hatch. If the rate on your fixed annuity drops by a certain amount, you can move your money to another company without owing any surrender charges.

1. One that pays 6% for six years,

2. One that guarantees 5.75% for six years but allows the yield to rise if interest rates move up, and

3. One that has a 7% first-year rate along with a bailout clause guaranteeing a 5% minimum.

To get the mix that's most appealing ask anyone trying to sell you a fixed annuity for a complete list of the fixed annuities for sale, with details of all the significant contract terms.

STAY THE COURSE

What if you already own a fixed annuity where the yield has been lowered to unattractive levels? Chances are, a salesperson will offer you a new annuity with an 8% or a 9% first-year yield, enough to pay off the surrender charge from your old annuity.

Should you accept? Unless you're really being victimized in your existing annuity, stay put until the surrender period lapses. If you switch annuities you'll wind up paying a surrender charge on your old contract, without knowing how low your rate will be reset at after the first year of your new contract.

PLAYING THE MARKET

**APRIL
15 equity-
indexed
annuity**
fixed annuity in which your income is pegged to the performance of the stock market.

The top-selling fixed annuity now is the *equity-indexed annuity*. Such contracts pay a return pegged to a stock market index such as the S&P 500, but with a guaranteed minimum rate in case stocks slump.

Your return might be set at 50% of the return of the S&P 500 over the next five years, for example, with a 3% guaranteed return protecting you against a weak stock market.

Throughout the 1990s, the annual return of the S&P 500 was around 20% per year. Thus, a 50% equity-indexed annuity would pay 10%, if history repeats, far better than you're likely to do with a traditional fixed annuity.

On the downside, if the stock market retreats you'll earn a 3% return on your fixed annuity.

This trade-off may be attractive. However, if you're considering an equity-indexed annuity, read the contract carefully before you buy. Terms vary widely from one issuer to another.

SPREAD YOUR RISKS

Before investing, find out your state's insurance protections for deferred annuities and keep your accounts well below that level. (Many states insure annuity contracts in the same way that federal deposit insurance covers bank accounts.)

Suppose your state guarantees annuities up to $100,000. If so, invest no more than $70,000 in any one contract. This will permit future growth without going over the limit.

FLEX PLAN—THE CONWAY STRATEGY

Ever since a 1982 change in the tax law, investors buying deferred annuities have been at a disadvantage. The law changed annuity withdrawals from a FIFO (first in, first out) to a LIFO (last in, first out) basis, making them more taxing.

A Tax Court decision (in the 1998 Conway case) opened up planning opportunities for investors. One strategy is to execute a partial exchange, tax-free, and withdraw both earnings and principal from the original contract.

In the Penalty Box

Suppose you invested $100,000 in a variable annuity five years ago. You invested in a stock fund subaccount and, thanks to the bull market, that subaccount now is worth

$250,000. You'd like to get your hands on $60,000 in cash.

In this scenario, though, the first $150,000 (the amount of your earnings) that you withdraw is taxable. There also is a 10% penalty tax before age $59^1/_2$. Thus, you might have to take out $120,000 worth of earnings to net $60,000, leaving only $130,000 (your $250,000 contract value minus $120,000 in withdrawals) in the annuity.

The Conway Way

As suggested by the Tax Court in the Conway case, you could take $125,000 from your variable annuity and transfer the funds to another variable annuity. Now you'd have two $125,000 variable annuities.

Your original investment is deemed to be split pro rata between the two annuities you now own. That is, you now have a $50,000 basis ($100,000 divided by two) in each of two $125,000 annuities.

If you want to get your hands on $60,000, you could withdraw all $75,000 in earnings from the first annuity and clear perhaps $37,500 (50%) after paying tax and penalties. The next $22,500 would be a tax-free return of principal, leaving you with $27,500 in the original annuity.

In addition, you'd still have the second annuity, worth $125,000. Together, your two annuities would be worth $152,500 ($125,000 and $27,500), $22,500 more than with the original plan.

In essence, that was the strategy adopted by Conway. He withdrew money from one annuity and used it to buy a second, smaller annuity. Section 1035 of the tax code, which permits tax-free exchanges of annuities, was cited as the rationale for continued tax deferral.

(Section 1035 of the Internal Revenue Code permits the deferral of taxation of an insurance or annuity product while allowing the owner to invest in a new or improved product. Under Section 1035, no gain or loss will be recognized on the exchange of life insurance or annuity contracts for other "like kind" contracts. This rule effectively defers taxation of gain built up in the transferred product when it is rolled over into another, similar product.)

Taxpayer Tops IRS

The IRS disagreed with Conway's reasoning. Section 1035, the IRS asserted, requires a complete rather than a partial rollover for treatment as a tax-free exchange.

The Tax Court found that "neither Sec. 1035 nor the regulations" require the exchange of an entire annuity for a tax-free exchange. Before and after the exchange, the taxpayer was in exactly the same position, with the same amount invested and the same amount of contract value. Therefore, a partial rollover was upheld.

Plan Ahead

If you're interested in this strategy, keep these points in mind:

- ✔ Buy your new annuity from a different issuer or from the same issuer in two different calendar years. Otherwise, federal law requires multiple annuities to be treated as one contract.
- ✔ Even though a partial transfer may be tax-free, there might be surrender charges to pay to the first issuer, based on the terms of the contract.
- ✔ The new annuity likely will have new sales charges and surrender fees. Look into all the details before leaping into a partial rollover.

THE MARVELS OF MECs

A modified endowment contract (MEC, as in check) is a cross between an annuity and a life insurance policy. The forerunners of the MEC were the single-premium whole life and single-premium variable life insurance contracts popular in the 1980s. MECs, which can be fixed (CD-type) or variable (mutual fund–type), are typically funded with a single premium.

Like an annuity, a MEC's investment account grows tax-deferred. However, unlike an annuity, the death benefit paid by a MEC can be income-tax-free to the beneficiary.

Further, a MEC can be owned by an irrevocable trust without losing its tax-favored status, while an annuity cannot. Thus, an asset such as a MEC can be used to fund a family trust (discussed in Chapter 13).

In fact, a MEC is an ideal investment for implementing the *shrinking trust strategy*, as explained next.

> **APRIL 15** **shrinking trust strategy** a plan calling for a surviving spouse to spend one's own assets and those of own trust fund so that the children's trust fund (exempt from estate tax) can grow substantially.

SHRINKING TRUST, EXPANDING WEALTH

Family and marital trusts are frequently utilized in estate planning for married couples. The family trust (also known as a B trust) is set up to hold as much as $1 million in assets, which can be passed to the couple's children, free of estate tax. The marital trust (A trust) is set up to hold the remaining assets.

After the first spouse dies, the second spouse has full access to the A trust, but limited access to the B trust. This limited access prevents the B trust assets from being included in the surviving spouse's estate. Instead, B trust assets pass directly to the named heirs upon the second death.

The shrinking trust tactic maximizes the estate-tax-advantaged nature of B trust assets. While a surviving spouse will likely have the right to spend the income from both the A and the B trusts, the larger the pool of assets remaining in the A trust after the second death, the greater the estate tax owed. Conversely, neither the growth of nor the income earned from B trust assets will be subject to estate taxes upon the death of the surviving spouse.

Therefore, the shrinking trust principle suggests that the surviving spouse should shrink the principal in the A trust before depleting the B trust, in an effort to minimize the estate tax bill. If the B trust is less likely to be depleted, funding it with a tax-deferred asset such as a MEC makes sense.

Moreover, because a MEC is not subject to the same funding restrictions applicable to traditional life insurance policies, its cash value, and thus its death benefit, can grow substantially faster, offering a solid return for the ultimate beneficiaries of the B trust—your children.

Chapter

Investing through Insurance

When you buy *permanent life insurance*, a portion of each *premium* you pay covers the purchase of the death benefit. The remaining portion (the *cash value*) is actually an investment. But because the product is, in fact, life insurance, it has several tax-advantaged components:

1. An income-tax-free death benefit,
2. Income-tax-free accumulation of cash value,
3. Income-tax-free withdrawals from cash value, and
4. Income-tax-free loan treatment.

Unlike any other investment, life insurance has a self-completion feature. Typically, even if the insured dies during the first year of the contract, the entire death benefit will be paid.

In general, the death benefit proceeds from a life insurance contract are excludable from the beneficiary's gross income. Death benefit proceeds from single-premium, periodic-premium, or flexible-premium life insurance policies are received income-tax-free by the

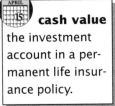

permanent life insurance
a policy that calls for relatively high initial premiums in order to keep the insurance in force as you grow older.

premium
payment for an insurance policy.

cash value
the investment account in a permanent life insurance policy.

beneficiary regardless of whether the beneficiary is an individual, a corporation, a partnership, a trustee, or an estate.

LIFE INSURANCE LOOPHOLES

The federal tax courts have also held that cash values built up inside an insurance policy are not constructively received by the policy owner unless they are distributed in exchange for surrender of the policy. Withdrawals from the cash account in a viable policy (one that meets the definition of life insurance as set forth in the Internal Revenue Code) are taxed according to the FIFO (first in, first out) accounting method, meaning they are included in gross income only to the extent they exceed the investment in the policy.

lapse
expiration of a life insurance policy for lack of premium payments. In a permanent life policy, income taxes will be triggered.

Distributions from the cash account of a viable policy that exceed the investment can be characterized as loans and thus also avoid income taxation. Upon *lapse* or surrender, the outstanding loan balance is automatically repaid from the policy proceeds held as collateral. (However, the use of collateralized policy values to repay a loan during lapse or surrender may cause the recognition of taxable income.)

The investment portion of permanent insurance, known as the cash account, grows dependent on the interest credited to the account by the insurance company. As a rule of thumb, a strong investment will be evidenced by cash-rich insurance.

AHEAD OF THE GAME

A cash-rich policy has a cash value equal to or greater than the total premiums paid. For example, if $10,000 in premiums have been paid for each of 10 years, the cash value should show at least $100,000 after 10 years. After 20 years, even though no further premium payments have been made, the cash account should equal or exceed $200,000.

The purpose of achieving a cash-rich policy is twofold:

1. The policy is more likely to hold together over the long haul without the infusion of additional cash.
2. The more cash in the cash account, the more tax-free funds are available to you.

PAYING THE PRICE

Given the aforementioned tax advantages, is life insurance really an attractive investment vehicle? Buying insurance can pay off in some circumstances, but only if you really know what you're buying.

With permanent life insurance, you're not only buying life insurance but you're paying extra premiums as well. A healthy 50-year-old male might be able to buy $200,000 worth of pure *term life insurance* with an annual premium of less than $500. To buy permanent life insurance, the annual premium might be $3,000, $4,000, or even greater each year.

 **term life insurance** pure life insurance, without an investment account.

Why would you want to spend even $3,000 for the same insurance you could buy for $500? Because the excess premium is channeled into an investment account, the cash value.

COVERAGE YOU WON'T OUTLIVE

The basic theory behind permanent life insurance is that the cash value will build up inside the policy and then, as you grow older and the cost of term insurance increases, money from the cash value can be used to keep the insurance in place. Thus, your life insurance may be truly permanent for you, no matter how old you are.

As mentioned, the cash value builds up inside the insurance policy free of income taxes. If you had invested in stocks or bonds or mutual funds instead, you'd owe tax each year on your dividends, interest, and capital gains. Therefore, you likely will be able to accumulate much more inside the policy than on the outside.

In addition, permanent life insurance policies allow you to borrow or withdraw money from the cash value, tax-free. There is a cost—the amount of life insurance will be reduced—but not necessarily an out-of-pocket cost.

The catch? You need to monitor your policy closely. If you borrow or withdraw too much from the cash value, the policy may terminate and all the income tax on the inside buildup will be due.

TAX-FREE BUILDUP

For example, suppose a 50-year-old pays a $10,000 life insurance premium every year for 15 years. The cash value buildup would depend on the investment return. If you assume, for example, that the investments earn 10% per year, which nets to around 8.5% to 9% after expenses, the $150,000 that's put in might grow to around $265,000 after 15 years.

If that is indeed the case, this individual could retire at age 65 and begin to withdraw and borrow around $26,500 per year from the policy. He or she might be able to do that for 16 years, pulling out a total of around $425,000, tax-free, on a $150,000 outlay—a ratio of nearly three to one.

At that point, there might be so little in the cash value that no more money could be pulled out. In this scenario, there would be a minimal death benefit, perhaps $70,000 to $75,000 at age 85 or 90. Further policy loans might cause the policy to terminate and generate a huge tax bill.

Another approach assumes the same 50-year-old makes the same $150,000 in premium payments and builds up the same $265,000 in cash value. Instead of withdrawing and borrowing $26,500 per year, assume he or she takes out $20,500 per year. This individual might be able to take that much tax-free cash out of the policy indefinitely. What's more, the death benefit might be much greater, around $300,000 at age 85 or 90.

READ THE FINE PRINT

Such examples are based on projections, not guarantees. Many factors, especially disappointing investment results, could change the picture. Nevertheless, it is possible to structure an insurance policy that provides tax-free cash to you as well as a substantial death benefit (again, free of income tax) to your loved ones.

TERM LIMITS

What about the expression that you're better off "buying term and investing the difference"? That may be a good strategy—but not always.

Assume that a 50-year-old male can pay an annual premium of $3,200 for a permanent life insurance policy with a death benefit of about $180,000. Alternatively, he could buy a $180,000 term policy with a lower premium and invest the difference.

Again, the outcome depends on investment results. Suppose you assume that all investments earn 10% but that the outside investments are taxed at 31% each year.

With these assumptions, buying term and investing the difference pays off for 11 years. After that, the investor is better off with the permanent life policy.

At age 65, for example, the investor would have nearly $55,000 in cash value within the insurance policy versus less than $45,000 in the outside investment account.

Either way, in addition, there would be $180,000 worth of insurance for the beneficiaries.

TIME-SENSITIVE

As this example points out, using life insurance as an investment makes sense only if you have a long time horizon. When you buy a permanent life insurance policy, commissions are paid to the agent in the first few years. Therefore, it takes a while to build up a substantial amount of cash value and realize the benefits of tax-free accumulation.

Assuming you have a time horizon of 15 years or longer, when does it make sense to use life insurance as an investment? Here are some possible scenarios:

✔ You're an employer who doesn't want to sponsor a retirement plan for your employees. You might use life insurance as a retirement plan that's solely for themselves.

✔ You participate in a retirement plan yet want to go beyond the limits you can contribute. Here, life insurance can serve as a supplement.

✔ You are very concerned about asset protection. In many states, life insurance policies can't be attached by a creditor. On the other hand, if you invest by buying stocks, bonds, or mutual funds, your investment portfolio may be vulnerable to creditors.

DEPICTING THE DRAWBACKS

Besides the requirement of a long holding period, what are the other drawbacks to using life insurance as an investment?

✔ *Investment commitment.* Investing through permanent life insurance locks you in to making substantial premium payments for a number of years. If you change your mind after a couple of payments, it's likely that there will be little in the way of cash value in the policy.

✔ *Tax perils.* The tax code says that an insurance policy bought with one or just a few payments will be considered a modified endowment contract (see Chapter 10), so tax-free withdrawals and loans won't be permitted.

✔ *Limited liquidity.* Even if you do make extended payments, qualifying for all the tax benefits of life insurance, you will not have tax-free access to all of your money. Enough cash value must be left in the policy to keep it in force and avoid a lapse. What's left in the policy eventually will go to your beneficiaries at your death.

SOONER OR LATER

Investing through life insurance may actually serve two purposes.

First, if you need the money in retirement, you can tap the cash value, tax-free. (However, life insurance cash value should be the last money you touch. You're better off going through your tax-deferred retirement accounts and your securities portfolio first, relying on your insurance as a backup.)

Secondly, if you don't need the cash value in your insurance policy, your heirs stand to receive a larger death benefit, free of income tax. Life insurance may serve double duty as an investment as long as you have loved ones you truly want to provide for after your death.

TAKING YOUR PICK

If you decide to use permanent life insurance as an investment vehicle, you need to decide which type of policy to use.

Traditional whole life and newer universal life policies offer a fixed rate of investment buildup similar to bond yields.

The latest version, variable life, offers several investment choices, known as subaccounts.

COVERAGE FOR YOUR WHOLE LIFE

Cash-rich policies typically come in two formats: whole life, and a variant of whole life known as universal life. These two formats offer differing options.

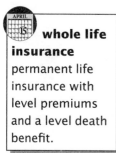

whole life insurance
permanent life insurance with level premiums and a level death benefit.

Traditional *whole life insurance* offers a level death benefit and a level premium. As long as premiums are paid and the policy performs as anticipated, neither the premium amount nor the death benefit will change.

What if the policy does not perform as well as expected (or as illustrated)? Then the death benefit and the premiums will remain the same but additional premiums will need to be paid over a longer time span than initially anticipated.

MASTERING THE UNIVERSAL

universal life insurance (UL)
permanent life insurance that offers flexibility in premium payments.

Conversely, *universal life insurance (UL)* offers either a level death benefit or an increasing death benefit. With the *increasing death benefit option*, your benefit increases in proportion to the increase in the policy's cash value.

Thus, if the investment portion of the policy performs successfully, your heirs receive the benefit in the form of an increased death benefit. On the other hand, should you need to decrease your premiums or death benefit, you also have this option.

 increasing death benefit option
an insurance policy where the death benefit increases along with any increase in the policy's cash value.

HOW THEY STACK UP

The additional flexibility of a universal life policy makes it an attractive investment. Even better, a UL policy is typically less expensive than its traditional whole life counterpart. However, the risk factor is greater for the UL investor than for the traditional whole life investor.

When a traditional whole life policy does not perform as well as expected, the worst thing that can happen (short of the company going bankrupt) is that the policy owner will have to pay premiums for additional years beyond those originally anticipated. When a universal life policy underperforms, however, there is the added risk that not only additional premiums but also larger premiums will be required.

THE UPS AND DOWNS OF VARIABLE LIFE

Would you like to invest in mutual funds yet never pay income tax? Consider a *variable life insurance* policy, which permits you to invest premium dollars in the stock market.

> **variable life insurance** permanent life insurance that offers investors the chance to direct premiums into stock funds, bond funds, and so on.

Many variable life policies impose sizable fees, though. Only time can overcome the up-front costs. Thus, you should plan to keep the policy in force indefinitely. The payoff may be retirement income for you and insurance benefits for your beneficiary.

The majority of variable products sold today are universal life products, structured like UL policies but with the cash accumulation invested according to the policyholders' direction in funds separate from the insurance company's general account.

SUBACCOUNTS IN SIGHT

Most variable life policies offer several investment choices, known as subaccounts. You can apportion your premium payments among these subaccounts and you can change your allocation if you desire.

Some of these subaccounts resemble mutual funds, others pay a fixed return, and still others offer diversified portfolios. Many variable life policies offer prime stock funds, international funds, specialty funds, and so on. If your subaccounts perform well, your cash value will swell.

On the other hand, it's possible to see subaccounts post negative returns, in which case your cash value will decline. (Generally, variable life policies have a minimum death benefit, which protects your beneficiary if your subaccounts lose money.)

Limited selection may be another concern. Even the broadest variable life policies have no more than a few dozen available subaccounts; most have just a handful. If you invest outside a variable life policy, you have thousands of mutual funds to choose among in addition to individual securities.

Stocking Up

As long as you're making a long-term commitment you should emphasize the subaccounts resembling stock funds, because stocks likely will provide the greatest long-term payoff. With a time horizon of 15 years or longer, well-managed variable life subaccounts should ride out any market corrections and deliver significant returns to investors.

TAX-FREE INCOME

When you want to tap your cash value, you can take tax-free withdrawals until you reach the amount of the money you've contributed. Then, you can take tax-free policy loans.

For example, suppose you pay $70,000 in premiums over seven years. After another eight years, your cash value is $150,000. Then you begin to withdraw $14,000 (less than 10% of your cash value) per year. The first five years, you're making withdrawals of the money you've contributed. Once you've withdrawn $70,000, you take policy loans.

Lapse-Proof

The best strategy is to keep policy loans to less than 10% of the cash value each year so the rest of your cash value balance can continue to grow. By monitoring your cash value closely, you can avoid a policy lapse that will trigger all the deferred income tax.

Moreover, keeping your policy in force guarantees that there will be a substantial payout to your beneficiary after your death.

WAY AHEAD OF INFLATION

Traditional universal life and whole life product returns are based on insurers' fixed accounts, which are mostly in investment-grade bonds. When adjusted for inflation, the real returns on these instruments over long periods of time (say, 50 years) are only about 2%.

When you look at common stock real returns, adjusted for inflation, they have measured about 8%. Thus, variable life policies probably will do better as long as a significant amount of the cash is invested in stock funds; it can be the best long-term accumulation product.

IN FOR THE LONG TERM

If you understand the nature of permanent life insurance pricing and the role played by interest rates, you can see that a variable product that generates significantly higher returns in the long run would also be an excellent product to meet long-term mortality needs. Even if you never tap the accumulation fund, the returns on that fund will likely allow for lower insurance costs over time.

Variable life products are regulated by the Securities and Exchange Commission (SEC). Therefore, although insurers can demonstrate high returns in a *policy illustration* they also are required to illustrate much lower results simultaneously. Finding a happy medium between these minimum and maximum projections may give you a valid expectation of future performance.

policy illustration computer-generated projection showing how a permanent life insurance policy may perform in the future.

SPLIT DECISIONS

Split dollar life insurance arrangements allow a business owner to enjoy the tax advantages of insurance while simultaneously lowering out-of-pocket policy costs.

✔ Under a split dollar agreement, a closely held or family business will advance the premiums to purchase permanent insurance.

✔ At the insured individual's death the company recovers the advance.

split dollar life insurance an arrangement in which an employer pays some or all of the premiums for insuring the life of an employee.

✔ The balance of the death benefit goes to the policy beneficiary (the surviving spouse, in many cases, or the co-owners of the business).

✔ If co-owners collect, the proceeds can be used to purchase the deceased owner's business interest, thus providing liquidity for the decedent's estate.

Economics Lesson

In most situations, the entire premium paid for ordinary life insurance is taxable to the covered employee (or else paid by the employee directly, with after-tax dollars). With a split dollar arrangement, however, only the *economic benefit* to the employee is taxable.

This benefit is calculated as the lesser of the "PS-58 cost" (an actuarially determined cost) or the cost of purchasing term insurance on the insured's life. As another option, a company can "bonus out" the PS-58 amount (and even the tax on that amount) thus making the expense deductible.

Questions have been raised about the IRS's reaction to split dollar arrangements, so you need to work with a knowledgeable professional when setting up this type of arrangement. If done properly, the actual cost to the insured individual can be quite reasonable.

 economic benefit
the value of insurance coverage obtained via a split dollar arrangement. This amount is taxable income to the covered employee.

Splitting into Reverse

A *reverse split dollar* arrangement reverses the parties of a normal split dollar agreement. The employee owns the policy but grants the employer the right to name itself as beneficiary for a specific portion of the death benefit. Depending on its design, a reverse split dollar plan can offer an additional advantage: funding retirement benefits with partially income-tax-free corporate dollars.

reverse split dollar
a split dollar arrangement in which the employee owns the policy but the company is named the beneficiary for a portion of the death benefit.

Doubling Up

It is also conceivable that a split dollar plan can double as a pension benefit plan set up to provide retirement income to employees. Here's one possible approach:

✔ Cash-rich life insurance can be applied for on the life of an executive.

✔ The policy may be owned by either the executive, the spouse, a co-owner of the company, or an irrevocable trust.

✔ The owner of the policy (known as the "assignor-owner") enters into a split dollar agreement with the company.

✔ The agreement assigns part of the policy's death benefit for use by the company.

The company frequently pays for its portion of the death benefit by making payments to a *prepaid premium account*. (This technique permits the company to budget level payments.)

Typically, the split dollar agreement provides that if the policy (or the executive's employment) is terminated prior to expiration of the agreement, the company can recover any values remaining in the unearned premium account but the remaining policy cash value balance belongs to the executive.

If the agreement expires while the policy is still in effect, the executive will likely own the entire cash value account and the death benefit.

Either way, the executive is entitled to take tax-free withdrawals from the policy cash value account to fund or supplement retirement income.

prepaid premium account
an arrangement in which an employer makes some split dollar payments in advance.

When You Invest in Yourself

Many "millionaires next door" achieved wealth by running their own business. If you're embarking on that path, one of your first decisions will be to choose a form of business ownership. Business entities are not created equal: To select among them you need to know the tax angles.

SOLE PROPRIETORSHIPS

Many small business owners prefer operating as a sole proprietor. Legal, accounting, and other administrative fees usually are lower for a *sole proprietorship* than those necessitated by other business forms. Organizational costs should be minimal and overall administration should be less complex.

sole proprietorship an unincorporated business run by a single individual.

Because income and deduction items are included on the owner's personal income tax return, business profits are taxed at the owner's individual rate. No additional tax return need be filed.

Unfortunately, tax considerations aside, the primary disadvantage associated with a sole proprietorship is the owner's unlimited personal liability to business creditors.

That is, all of your personal assets may be at risk from a claim for damages.

C CORPORATIONS, S CORPORATIONS, PARTNERSHIPS, AND LLCs

Indeed, in today's litigious society, business owners make inviting targets. If one customer trips on your premises or your delivery van is involved in an accident, you can expect to be sued. What's more, no matter how frivolous the claim, you might lose a huge judgment. Even a settlement could bankrupt you.

To protect yourself against such disasters, you need a business structure that provides limited liability. Traditionally, business owners have incorporated their companies to gain limited liability. If you decide to incorporate, you have two options:

1. C corporation
2. S corporation

The regular corporate structure is a *C corporation*. There are advantages, tax and nontax, to operating a C corporation:

✔ Fringe benefits, especially health insurance, may be deductible.

✔ Lenders often prefer working with C corporations.

✔ You have a great deal of flexibility when it comes to succession planning.

C corporation a business entity offering limited liability to shareholders. C corporations must pay a corporate income tax.

ZERO CAN BE A MINUS FOR C CORPORATIONS

C corporations have to file corporate tax returns and pay tax on any income. Therefore, many closely held C corporations zero out taxable income by paying bonuses to owner-employees.

Often, that's a mistake. Chances are that you're in a 31%, 36%, even 39.6% personal federal tax bracket. Every dollar your C corporation pays to you will be taxed at your high personal tax rates.

Leave Something on the Plate

The better way: Every C corporation should attempt to keep $50,000 to $75,000 in taxable profits each year. Generally, the first $50,000 will be taxed at only 15% while the next $25,000 faces a 25% tax rate. Why pay tax at higher rates?

What's more, if you zero out your corporate tax return, you're telling the IRS, "I'm playing games with taxable income." You can expect an audit.

On the other hand, you'll likely escape an audit if you show some taxable income. The IRS likes the idea of collecting something from your corporation, in addition to the personal income tax you have to pay.

Cash in the Company

Suppose your C corporation nets $50,000 and pays $7,500 in tax to the IRS. What should you do with the other $42,500? Don't pay dividends. Such payouts are taxable to the recipients but not deductible by the corporation.

You can invest the money, perhaps earning tax-deferred or tax-exempt interest. However, you must have a good reason (such as plans for future expansion) for building up funds inside your corporation. Otherwise, the IRS may hit your company with a steep accumulated earnings tax.

You can borrow the money, tax-free, from your company. Just be sure you formalize the loan and make regular interest payments back to the company, eventually repaying the loan. Otherwise, the IRS will call the whole transaction a sham and tax it as a dividend.

Buy tax-favored life insurance. This solution may be the simplest; it also avoids the tax problems of accumulated earnings and "constructive" dividends, which the

IRS will tax as dividends even though you call them by another name, such as loan interest.

S MAY STAND FOR SAVVY

 S corporation
a business entity offering the liability protection of a corporation without the need to pay the corporate income tax. Any corporate profits are taxed to the shareholders as personal income.

 **employee stock ownership plan (ESOP)**
a retirement plan in which ownership of a company is transferred to employees.

Not every business should operate as a C corporation; sometimes an *S corporation* structure is better. With an S corporation, all profits and losses flow through to shareholders, so there's no corporate income tax to pay.

You need to meet certain tests to qualify for S corporation status, but those rules were eased a bit in 1996: S corporations now can have as many as 75 shareholders, they can include pension funds and *employee stock ownership plans (ESOPs)* as shareholders, and they can own subsidiaries.

Here are some circumstances in which an S corporation makes sense:

✔ You expect a new business to post start-up losses. The losses can be passed through to the owners, who may be able to deduct them.

✔ You expect to sell your company. Gain on sale of an S corporation will be taxed only once while C corporation sales are double-taxed.

✔ You have teenage children and you intend to do some family income-shifting.

Tax-Bracket Arbitrage

To help you understand the possible benefits, here's one possible scenario:

Bill and Betty Williams are married, the only shareholders in Williams Corp., an S corporation. In 2000, Williams Corp. earns $450,000, all of which is paid to Bill as salary and bonus.

To cut taxes, Bill could pay himself a $100,000 salary as long as he can demonstrate that's comparable to the earnings of other top executives at similar companies. The other $350,000 would be considered corporate earnings, taxable to Bill and Betty on their joint tax return.

> **APRIL 15**
>
> **Tax Tip**   Shifting $350,000 from earned to un-earned income would save more than $10,000 in Medicare tax, assessed at 2.9% for employer and employee.

Even better results could have been accomplished by shifting shares in the company to their two children. Between them, Bill and Betty can transfer up to $20,000 worth of shares each year to each child, without incurring any gift tax. Using discounts for illiquidity and lack of control, they can make relatively large gifts.

Say that Williams Corp. has 1 million shares outstanding and is valued at $1 million. If Bill and Betty want to transfer $20,000 worth of shares to their son Ted, they might say that each share is worth $1 and transfer 20,000 shares.

However, 20,000 shares (2% of the outstanding shares) really aren't worth $20,000 (2% of the company) on the market. No outsider would pay that much, considering the lack of a voice in corporate policy and the uncertainty of finding a buyer for the closely held shares.

Therefore, Bill and Betty can hire an appraiser who might say that 30,000 shares would be worth $20,000 to an outsider. If so, they can give Ted 30,000 shares.

By using this strategy, they might succeed in giving Ted and his sister Theresa a total of 300,000 shares in five years. Now, the children will own 30% of the company.

In that case, if Williams Corp. shows a $350,000 corporate profit, $105,000 (30%) will be income to Ted and Theresa. If the kids are in a 28% tax bracket, rather than the 39.6% Bill and Betty pay on a joint return, that's an income tax saving of over $12,000. If Ted and Theresa are in a 15% bracket, the annual income tax savings will be more than $25,000.

In many states, income tax savings would be even greater. Moreover, the income tax savings are in addition to the aforementioned payroll tax savings.

Kid Stuff

S corporation earnings are considered unearned income. Children under age 14 can have only $1,400 worth of favorably taxed unearned income per year (in 2000); larger amounts are taxed at the parents' rates. Thus, this strategy will have the greatest payoff after your children reach age 14.

Note, in this example, that Bill and Betty still control Williams Corp., with 70% of the shares. Thus, they can decide how much, if any, of the corporate earnings to distribute to shareholders and how much to keep in the corporation. Income tax will be owed regardless of whether dividends are distributed.

 Tax Tip   Transferring S corporation shares to your kids will have estate tax advantages, too. In this example, Bill and Betty have removed 30% of the corporation's value from their taxable estates without incurring any gift tax.

MULTIPLE CHOICE

You may not have to make a choice between an S or a C corporation. Often, business owners have more than one corporation, C and S. They even can have some business operated as a sole proprietorship, for purposes such as paying deductible wages to their children. (For a sole proprietorship, children under 18 are not subject to Social Security, Medicare, or unemployment taxes.)

limited liability company (LLC) a business entity combining the protection of a corporation with the tax planning opportunities of a partnership.

LEARNING TO LOVE LLCs

A relatively new business form, *limited liability companies (LLCs)* offer asset protection, favorable taxation, and fewer restrictions than S corporations. Therefore, LLCs have become an increasingly popular form of enterprise for these reasons:

✔ All the owners can protect their personal assets from business liability, as they can if they form a corporation.

✔ LLCs are taxed like *partnerships*, which may be very favorable: no corporate income tax, flow-through of losses, and so on.

✔ LLCs offer the chance to make special allocations if there are multiple owners.

✔ An LLC can have a foreign owner but an S corporation can't.

✔ LLC owners can increase their basis by including their share of business liabilities. This may mean larger loss deductions and larger tax-free distributions.

✔ When appreciated property is distributed by an LLC to its owners, tax isn't due until each owner sells the property. With an S corporation, the distribution generates a taxable gain.

✔ Favorable transfer tax valuations may be used. Because many LLC agreements restrict transfers, interests may be given or bequeathed to loved ones at a substantial discount for gift and estate tax purposes.

partnership
an unincorporated business with two or more principals. The opportunity to allocate income among partners leads to planning opportunities.

On the other hand, S corporations may be preferable in some situations:

✔ If your compensation is below the maximum amount subject to Social Security taxes ($76,200 in 2000), you'll pay lower taxes with an S corporation than with an LLC.

✔ If you're planning to acquire and liquidate another corporation, an S corporation can do this tax-free but the transaction will be taxable if done by an LLC.

deemed liquidation
tax trap that companies may fall into when switching from one business entity to another. Paper profits may be generated, leading to a tax obligation.

limited partner
a partner who enjoys limited liability and makes no operating decisions.

family limited partnership (FLP)
a partnership where senior family members usually act as general partners, in control of the assets. Ownership of those assets can be shifted to younger family members, who are limited partners.

✔ If you operate in several states, each state may require separate LLC filings, using different rules, while S corporation filings usually are simpler.

✔ If you are seriously concerned about protecting your personal assets, be aware that although LLCs theoretically provide shelter, they're too new to have a track record in this area. S corporations have proven over the years that they can provide liability protection. Some attorneys feel more comfortable with precedents on their side.

An LLC is often the first choice of entity when starting a new business. If your company already is in existence, IRS regulations make it relatively easy to change entities.

However, you should be cautious about switching from S corporation to LLC status. Such changes frequently lead to a *deemed liquidation*, triggering gains on corporate-owned assets.

NOT YOUR FATHER'S PARTNERSHIP

Regular general partnerships offer a great deal of tax flexibility but no protection of your personal assets from business creditors. To remedy this defect, several types of specialized partnerships have been developed.

In limited partnerships, general partners run the business and bear all the liability. *Limited partners* are passive investors with no liability beyond the cash they contribute and any notes they sign. Limited partnerships are frequently used to own and operate real estate.

Family limited partnerships (FLPs) (see Chapter 13) permit you to transfer 99% of your assets to your children and grandchildren at a steep *valuation discount*, yet still control those assets as a 1% general partner. Therefore, they're excellent vehicles for estate planning and asset protection.

First cousin to the LLC, the *limited liability partnership (LLP)* form has been adopted by leading professional firms. LLPs protect each partner's personal assets from exposure to the misdeeds of other partners or employees. In some states this protection is limited to malpractice claims while in others it includes protection from trade creditors as well.

If you're already in any type of a partnership—such as one formed to hold investment property—you should consider an LLP conversion.

MIXING BUSINESS WITH PLEASURE

No matter why type of business structure you choose, you're likely to do some traveling and entertaining. When you know the rules, you'll find that the IRS will share some of those costs.

Tax law requires you to maintain records for business travel and entertainment; generally, estimation of these expenses is not permitted.

Fortunately, record keeping for most business travel is not difficult, assuming you use credit cards to pay for airfares, hotel rooms, car rentals, restaurant meals, and so forth. If you minimize the use of cash to pay for deductible expenses, a canceled check or a credit card slip can refresh your recollection regarding expenditures. You may want to keep one credit card solely for business expenditures, which will help you keep your records straight.

Credit card receipts and canceled checks may show how much you spent, and when, but they won't indicate why the expenditures were made. For an expense to be deductible, you must have some record showing the business purpose of that expense or the business benefit derived (or expected to be derived) as a result of the expenditure.

 **valuation discount**
a reduction in the expressed value of an asset transferred to a family member, who lacks control over that asset. Such discounts may save gift or estate tax.

limited liability partnership (LLP)
a business entity similar to an LLC, available to organizations such as professional service firms that may choose partnership status.

Tax Tip Your simplest strategy is to make a note on the back of your credit card receipt.

More or Less

If you fly to another city for a four-day business trip, your travel and hotel deductions probably will be sustained. Suppose, however, you decide to take a three-day vacation at the same hotel, extending your stay there.

Because you devoted more time (four days) to business than to pleasure (three days), your airfare likely will be deductible. Most of your hotel bills also will be deductible, although your tax preparer might advise you not to deduct the cost of the additional stay.

As long as your trip is primarily for business you can get a partial deduction for restaurant meals, too. When you're traveling away from home on business, meals qualify as business meals even if you eat your meals alone or with persons who are not connected with your business. However, only 50% of the cost of business meals may be deducted.

The same is true for business-related entertainment and beverages served apart from meals. Thus, if you treat a client to drinks and a night at a ball game, running up a $100 tab, only $50 can be deducted.

 Tax Tip   You don't need receipts for expenditures under $75, although you should have some documentation. If you take a business trip and keep a log, you might be able to take reasonable deductions for cabs, tips, dry cleaning, and so on, even if you don't have receipts for every expense. If it's not practical to keep track of such incidentals, you can make feasible estimates.

Another alternative is to use the federal per diem rates. In certain high-cost areas those rates are now $185 per day, meaning you're allowed to deduct that much for meals, lodging, and incidentals without having receipts for each individual item.

Saturday Night Specials

Increasingly, travelers plan their trips so that they stay over a Saturday night, in order to get a lower airfare. If that's the case, you likely will be able to deduct at least some of your weekend expenses. Thus, if you attend a conference where the meetings begin on Monday, you most likely can arrive the previous Friday or Saturday and write off your travel and hotel costs, even if you spend the weekend on the golf course. However, the math must be credible: The IRS will be skeptical if you run up an extra $500 in weekend costs in order to save $300 in airfare.

Property Pointers

You may have other opportunities to mix business with pleasure, especially if you own investment property in a distant area. If you'd like to write off travel costs incurred to examine your real estate, you can call your local property manager in advance to arrange an appointment for an on-site inspection. Make formal arrangements and confirm them by letter or fax, keeping all of the correspondence in a file.

After your return home, follow up with another fax or letter to summarize the results of your visit. The more businesslike you are, the greater the chances of sustaining your deductions.

Spouse Trap

Although your own airfare will be deductible if you take a trip that's primarily for business, deducting your spouse's expenses may be more difficult. In order for those outlays to be deductible, your spouse must be on your payroll, with a genuine business reason for taking the trip. There might be nontechnical sessions to attend, for example.

Putting your spouse on the payroll may have other benefits. Under recent changes in tax law, employing your spouse may increase the family's contributions to a retirement plan. However, extra payroll taxes will be due, so you'll have to carefully weigh the costs versus the benefits.

If your spouse isn't an employee, his or her airfare won't be deductible but you won't have to settle for deducting half the hotel bill. Suppose, for example, you pay $220 for a double room that would have cost one person $185; you can deduct $185 rather than $110, half the cost of the room. Therefore, you should ask your hotel for a room rate schedule showing its single rates for the days you're there.

Similarly, airport cab rides you take with your spouse will be fully deductible if you would have paid the same amount as a single passenger. In addition, you probably can write off your spouse's share of entertainment costs if he or she accompanied you during a meal while you entertained business associates. Again, there's a 50% limit to this deduction.

Party Plan

You may be able to take your spouse—or any companion—on a business trip and enjoy tax breaks, even without hiring your companion. If you operate your practice as a corporation, the corporation may be able to deduct its outlays attributable to you, as an employee, while neither you nor your companion has to report the reimbursement as taxable income. To accomplish this, there must be a bona fide business purpose for your companion's presence on the trip.

Suppose, for example, you attend an industry conference where you plan to throw a small party for prospective clients. If all of the other people will have spouses or significant others, you'd need a companion, too, so you won't feel out of place. Thus, you could bring your companion to the conference and have your corporation reimburse you for the expenses you incur. In the opinion of some tax pros, you have grounds for not including such reimbursements in your taxable income.

Similar tactics may apply to business meals and country club dues. Your corporation could reimburse you for your outlays, taking a 50% deduction for the meals and no deduction for the club dues. Ordinarily, you'd have to include all the club dues reimbursement and half of the meals reimbursements in your taxable income, but that won't be the case if the meals and your club activities were related to your business.

Foreign Affairs

Special rules apply for business trips outside the United States. Generally, all costs, including transportation, must be allocated between the business and personal portions of your trip. There are some exceptions, though. If your major reason for taking the trip was not a holiday or a vacation, you can take a 100% travel write-off and deduct a substantial share of other costs. You should keep a file showing that the major reason for taking a trip was business-related.

There's also a "one-week rule": Your travel expenses will be fully deductible if you are out of the country less than seven days. Suppose, for example, you travel to England on a business matter. You can spend a few days sightseeing and still write off the airfare as long as you return within a week.

There is a catch, though, when it comes to attending foreign conventions. For expenses to be deductible you must show that it was "as reasonable" for the meeting to be held outside North America as within it. Thus, if you attend a conference overseas, be sure to load up on documentation about the sponsor, the subject matter, the attendees, and other details to show that there truly was a healthy dose of business in the business-pleasure mix.

Remember when you prepare your tax return that travel and entertainment deductions are likely to attract IRS scrutiny, especially if they're sizable in relation to your income. Take legitimate deductions, by all means, but take only those deductions for which you have a pile of paperwork to prove you weren't just playing.

Chapter

Minimize the Cruelest Tax

Taxes on capital gains are usually assessed at 20%, while the highest federal income tax bracket hits 39.6%. Neither, however, can compete with federal estate and gift taxes, which currently reach 55% (a 60% effective rate, in some situations). Fortunately, several estate planning strategies are available to lessen the negative impact.

UNIFIED TRANSFER CREDIT

The federal estate and gift taxes are graduated, beginning at 18% and sliding all the way up to 55% for estates that exceed $3 million. (See Figure 13.1.)

Fortunately, the tax code entitles each taxpayer to a tax credit known as the *unified transfer credit* because estate and gift tax rates are now the same. (Both gift and estate taxes are calculated based on the same tax brackets.) The unified transfer credit can be used to shelter assets from either gift or estate taxes.

This credit can exempt a taxable estate of $675,000 to $1 million from estate tax, depending on the year of death. If two individuals are married, each can use his or

> **unified transfer credit** an offset against gift and estate tax. Each individual's credit shelters $675,000 worth of tax in 2000, an amount that will rise gradually to $1 million in 2006.

FIGURE 13.1 Unified Federal Gift and Estate Tax		
Taxable Gift or Estate	Tax	Rate on Excess
$ 500,000— $ 750,000	$ 155,800	37%
$ 750,000— $ 1,000,000	$ 248,300	39%
$ 1,000,000— $ 1,250,000	$ 345,800	41%
$ 1,250,000— $ 1,500,000	$ 448,300	43%
$ 1,500,000— $ 2,000,000	$ 555,800	45%
$ 2,000,000— $ 2,500,000	$ 780,800	49%
$ 2,500,000— $ 3,000,000	$1,025,800	53%
$ 3,000,000— $10,000,000	$1,290,800	55%
$10,000,000—$20,000,000		60%
$20,000,000+		55%

$1,000,000+ To Grandchildren (GSTT = 55% Twice) 80%

her unified transfer credit to pass a total of $2 million (assuming they both die after 2005) to the next generation, free of estate tax.

One of the more popular and effective methods to assure utilization of both spouses' unified credits involves implementation of "A/B trust provisions."

TWIN TRUSTS

 unlimited marital deduction tax benefit allowing one spouse to give or bequeath any amount to the other spouse, tax-free.

A/B trust provisions can be included within a will or a living trust. This trust structure is designed to provide a surviving spouse with access to the family's accumulated wealth while simultaneously minimizing the combined federal estate tax bills due upon the death of both spouses.

To accomplish these ambitious goals it is necessary to utilize both spouses' lifetime unified transfer credits while concurrently taking advantage of the *unlimited marital deduction*, which provides for tax-free interspousal transfers of property.

A/B trust provisions create two trusts:

1. The *B trust*, also known as the family trust, is designed to hold an amount equal to what the decedent's unified transfer credit can shelter from estate tax ($675,000 to $1 million, depending on the year of death).

2. The *A trust*, also known as the marital trust, is created to hold the remaining estate assets, transferred at the death of the first spouse for the benefit of the surviving spouse, via the unlimited marital deduction.

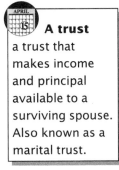

B trust a trust in which assets are left to the next generation. Also known as a family trust.

A trust a trust that makes income and principal available to a surviving spouse. Also known as a marital trust.

BYPASSING THE IRS

Although the surviving spouse may control the A trust and have complete access to both its income and principal, he or she also may have access to the income from the B trust as well as a limited right to invade the B trust principal. This technically limited access to the B trust assets prevents their inclusion in the surviving spouse's estate at the second death.

Instead, the B trust assets are treated as if they pass from the first spouse directly to the children (bypassing, for tax purposes only, the surviving spouse). Because the B trust assets transfer to the next generation free of estate taxes, thanks to usage of the first spouse's unified transfer credit, the surviving spouse's own unified transfer credit remains available to shelter an additional $675,000 to $1 million from estate tax at the time of the second death.

If each spouse leaves $1 million to the children (after 2005), a total of $2 million can be passed on, tax-free.

UNLIMITED MARITAL ESTATE TAX DEDUCTION

The 1981 tax law allows unlimited property to transfer from a deceased spouse to the surviving spouse, free of estate tax. By postponing any tax until the survivor's death, this unlimited marital deduction effectively delays estate tax until a married couple's property transfers to the next generation.

Although most estate plans make use of this deduction, transferring all property to a surviving spouse will not necessarily achieve the most advantageous tax result. Why not? Because if the surviving spouse owns all the marital property it will be taxed in his or her estate at death, with only one unified credit to shelter it.

Instead, the unlimited marital deduction is best used in conjunction with tax exemptions available to both spouses (such as the unified credit) to transfer the maximum amount of wealth to the next generation.

UNLIMITED SPOUSAL GIFTS

One spouse also can make unlimited lifetime gifts to the other spouse, tax-free. The catch? Recipients of lifetime gifts also receive the donor's cost basis, meaning they may owe capital gains tax when they sell. Inherited assets get a basis step-up, effectively eliminating the tax on prior appreciation.

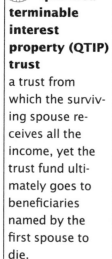

qualified terminable interest property (QTIP) trust
a trust from which the surviving spouse receives all the income, yet the trust fund ultimately goes to beneficiaries named by the first spouse to die.

Although tax savings are usually the primary motivation for use of either unlimited marital deduction, other factors should be addressed as well. In particular, the needs of the surviving spouse may require that more property pass to him or her than what is dictated purely by the tax ramifications. That is, if the first spouse to die leaves $675,000 to $1 million to the children, the survivor may not have enough money to live comfortably.

QTIP TRUSTS

Qualified terminable interest property (QTIP) trusts are similar to A trusts: One spouse can leave property to the other spouse for lifetime use, free of estate taxes. Unlike an A trust, however, a QTIP does not give the surviving spouse the right to determine who shall inherit the trust funds upon his or her death. Instead, the QTIP trustee will control distribution of the funds remaining as set forth by the terms of the trust.

A QTIP trust is particularly useful in situations where a second marriage has occurred and one spouse has children from a previous marriage. That is, the surviving spouse can be the immediate heir of the decedent's estate but the children from the first marriage will be the ultimate beneficiaries.

ANNUAL $10,000 GIFT TAX EXCLUSION

Gift taxes are subject to the same graduated rates as estate taxes. Nonetheless, the tax code provides an *annual gift tax exclusion* that allows any donor to give up to $10,000 in money or property to each donee, each year, free of gift tax.

For example, a father can give $10,000 to each of his three children, for five years (for a total of $150,000) without the imposition of any gift tax.

Under current law, the annual gift tax exclusion will be indexed to inflation, increasing in $1,000 increments. Thus, by approximately 2002, the limits for the gift tax exclusion will increase to $11,000 apiece, or $22,000 for a married couple.

VALUING CRUMMEY GIFTS

To qualify for this exclusion the gift must be either an outright gift or a gift of a present interest.

So-called *Crummey trusts* take advantage of the $10,000 annual gift tax exclusion to fund a trust free of gift taxes. A Crummey trust (named after a 1968 court decision) is an *irrevocable trust* that authorizes the trust beneficiaries, for a limited period of time, to withdraw a portion of the trust principal.

Whether a beneficiary makes the withdrawal is irrelevant. The fact that the withdrawal right exists is enough to qualify funds transferred by the donor to the trust as a

 **annual gift tax exclusion** tax benefit allowing gifts to be made, tax-free. Currently, each person can give away up to $10,000 per recipient per year.

 Crummey trust a trust accepting gifts that qualify for the annual gift tax exclusion. To do so, the beneficiaries must be given the right to withdraw these gifts.

irrevocable trust a trust that cannot be canceled or significantly changed.

present interest gift, even though the beneficiaries may not enjoy their interest for years to come.

GENERATION-SKIPPING TRANSFER TAX EXEMPTION

A generation-skipping gift passes from a transferor to (or for the benefit of) a recipient who is two or more generations younger than the transferor. Thus, gifts or bequests from grandparent to grandchild are subject to this tax.

The generation-skipping transfer (GST) tax is currently 55%. Therefore, a generation-skipping gift will be subject to the estate tax and to the generation-skipping transfer tax. Because a tax of 55%, imposed twice, equals an 80% tax, a generation-skipping gift that falls into the highest estate tax bracket will leave as little as 20% of the original gift for the recipient.

However, the tax code provides every taxpayer with a generation-skipping transfer tax exemption of $1 million that can be allocated to property of his or her choosing. The exemption can either be allocated by the transferor (or an executor) on a tax return or be automatically allocated by a formula dictated by the IRS.

Beginning in 1999, the $1 million exemption from the generation-skipping transfer tax is increased each year in $10,000 increments to keep pace with inflation. (As of this writing, the exemption is $1.01 million.)

This $1 million exemption can prove particularly valuable when used in conjunction with a trust. Suppose you transfer $1 million to a *generation-skipping transfer trust* established for the benefit of your grandchildren. You could allocate your generation-skipping transfer tax exemption at the time of transfer.

Over the next 20 years, the trust principal might grow to $5 million; at your death, the trust fund would be distributed to the beneficiaries. Because you allocated your tax exemption at the date of transfer to the trust, no generation-skipping transfer tax should be due on any part of the $5 million received by your grandchildren.

generation-skipping transfer trust
a trust created to pass assets to grandchildren and even great-grandchildren while minimizing transfer taxes.

FAMILY BUSINESS AND FAMILY FARM EXCLUSION

Tax legislation passed in 1997 created a new estate tax exclusion for qualified family-owned businesses and family farms. This *family business and farm exclusion* is equal to the difference between $1.3 million and the unified credit exemption equivalent in effect at the time of death.

In 2000, for example, this exemption is $675,000, so the bonus estate exclusion for family business or farm owners who have died in 2000 is $625,000: $1.3 million minus $675,000. Subsequently, the universal exemption will gradually increase to $1 million in 2006 and thereafter, reducing this estate tax break to $300,000.

To qualify for this bonus estate tax relief, several conditions must be satisfied:

family business and farm exclusion a tax benefit allowing a family business or farm to shelter more of its value from estate tax than would be the case with other types of assets.

✔ The value of the decedent's business or farm interests, including prior gifts, must exceed 50% of the decedent's adjusted gross estate.

✔ At least 50% of the business or farm must be owned by the decedent and members of his or her family. Alternatively, at least 70% must be owned by members of two families or at least 90% must be owned by the members of three families. If two or three families are involved, at least 30% of the business or farm must be owned by the decedent and decedent's family.

✔ A family member must materially participate in the business or farm for 10 years after the decedent's death. If this condition is not satisfied during the first six years, there's a 100% recapture of the estate tax savings, plus interest. For the next four years, there's a 20% annual phaseout. There are no exceptions or hardship provisions to this test.

This tax break was modified by a 1998 change in the law. Now, family businesses are entitled to a $675,000 deduction, no matter when death occurs; if you use the deduction, you must subtract it from $1.3 million to get your maximum estate tax exemption.

For example, suppose Joe Jones dies in 2006 and his estate claims a $675,000 family business deduction. His estate tax exemption is capped at $625,000 ($1.3 million minus $675,000). If the estate claims a family business deduction of $500,000, the estate tax exemption would be $800,000 ($1.3 million minus $500,000).

This latter may be a better deal because a deduction reduces the size of the taxable estate. In effect, it comes off the top, where estate tax rates are highest.

By contrast, the estate tax exemption shelters assets at the bottom of the estate tax table. The effect of the new law might be, say, to shift taxable estate assets from a 55% to a 41% bracket.

Assume death after 2005, an estate worth $2.5 million, and the maximum $675,000 family business deduction; the 1998 law would save $33,000 in estate tax, versus the 1997 version.

The exclusion for a family business or farm is an estate tax break but not a gift tax break. Planning to take advantage of this tax break is extremely complicated, so be certain you develop an estate plan by consulting with qualified professionals.

CHARITABLE REMAINDER TRUSTS

A charitable remainder trust, or CRT, is an irrevocable trust with two sets of beneficiaries: (1) you and your spouse are typically the income beneficiaries, and (2) qualified charities are the ultimate remainder beneficiaries. You also fulfill the roles of creator (by funding the trust) and, if you choose, trustee.

The Taxpayer Relief Act of 1997 added restrictions on charitable remainder trusts:

First, the annual payout cannot be set at a rate to exceed 50%.

Second, charitable remainder trusts must have a projected residual value of at least 10% (i.e., at least 10% of the original contribution must be projected to go to charity at the end of the trust term, based on current interest rate levels). This may cause young donors to set low payouts to the income beneficiaries; it may even prevent extremely young (under age 35) donors from setting up charitable remainder trusts with lifetime payouts.

If they're unencumbered by debt, highly appreciated assets can be transferred to the trust, where they can be sold without paying capital gains taxes. The full value of the transferred assets can then be reinvested, and you, as an income beneficiary, can immediately reap the results.

Over your lifetime (or, if you choose, for a set period of years) you will receive a payout expressed either as a percentage of the assets contributed or as a percentage of trust assets, revalued annually. At death, the remainder goes to charity.

Because these assets go directly to charity upon your death, they are not taxed in your estate. Furthermore, you will receive a charitable income tax deduction, based on the present value of the charitable remainder interest. Therefore, if implemented properly, this strategy should provide increased income to you (based on circumvention of the capital gains tax), an income tax deduction, and lower estate taxes.

CHARITABLE LEAD TRUSTS

With a CRT (discussed in the previous section), the transferor (or family members) retains an income interest in the property for a specified period of time, after which the assets belong irrevocably to the charity. A *charitable lead trust (CLT)* simply reverses this pattern of deferred giving. With a CLT, a charitable organization receives the income generated by assets transferred to a trust over a set period of time, with the remainder interest (what's left after the period expires) either reverting back to the donor or passing to a noncharitable beneficiary such as a child or grandchild.

The act of giving an income interest in the trust's

charitable lead trust (CLT) a trust that pays certain amounts to charity for a certain time period, then distributes the assets to individual beneficiaries.

assets to a charitable beneficiary generates an estate tax deduction, which can substantially reduce the donor's overall estate tax liability.

Further, the set period of time between the trust's inception and distribution of the trust's assets to the non-charitable beneficiary (the grandchildren, for example) can allow the donor to leverage the use of the unified credit and the generation-skipping transfer tax exclusion to transfer more assets to heirs, free of taxes. This leverage occurs because estate/GST liability is calculated based on the present value of this future gift.

QUALIFIED PERSONAL RESIDENCE TRUSTS

It's likely that your home is among your largest single assets. The transfer of that home to your children (whether today or at the time of your death) may use up most, if not all, of your $675,000 to $1 million lifetime exemption from gift and estate tax.

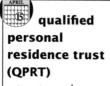

qualified personal residence trust (QPRT) a trust used to pass a residence to the next generation at a low gift-tax value.

Fortunately, there is a way to minimize the estate tax burden on the transfer of your home while maximizing the power of your unified credit. A *qualified personal residence trust (QPRT)* allows you to transfer either your principal residence or vacation home (or both) to your children with little tax liability, even as you continue to reside there.

As the grantor of the QPRT, you transfer your home to the trust but retain an interest in that home for a term of years. (Thus, you are also known at the term holder.) At expiration of the term the property passes to your children (the remainder beneficiaries).

Using a QPRT allows you to move the entire value of your home, including any future growth, outside of your estate (as long as you survive the term) and thus beyond the reach of estate taxes. Nonetheless, because your children are remainder beneficiaries, the IRS calculates the value of your gift by determining the present value of that future gift.

As a result, the gift to your children is only a fraction of your home's fair market value, and will require a correspondingly lower utilization of your unified credit to pass it to the next generation, free of estate taxes. (Your annual $10,000 gift tax exclusion is inapplicable to this strategy because you are making a gift of a future interest to your children.)

PRIVATE FAMILY FOUNDATIONS

Private family foundations are privately funded, privately controlled organizations created to contribute to various charitable causes. The private family foundation may be your ideal estate planning strategy if your objectives include:

> **private family foundation** a charitable entity established to allow the creator and successors to control future donations.

1. Contributing to a charitable cause and taking a tax deduction without relinquishing all control over your gift.
2. Minimizing your estate tax liability.
3. Avoiding capital gains tax on the sale of appreciated property contributed to charity.
4. Providing continuing employment and activity for your family members.
5. Identifying and preserving your family name.

Charitable giving through a private family foundation yields two substantial income tax benefits:

First, if you contribute appreciated property to your foundation, your foundation may sell that property without paying capital gains tax.

Second, you get an immediate tax deduction for up to 30% of your adjusted gross income (20% for appreciated property). Any charitable income tax deduction not used in your contribution year may be carried forward over the next five years.

You may also arrange for your children, grandchildren,

and even more distant descendants to receive salaries as employees of your foundation by naming them as replacement trustees or directors, to succeed you after your death or resignation.

A private family foundation must distribute at least 5% of its assets each year to public charities. That is, if you leave $2 million to your private family foundation, at least $100,000 (5% of $2 million) must go to recognized charities.

However, any earnings in excess of 5% per year can be used for legitimate expenses, including salaries for your descendants as directors of your foundation.

FAMILY LIMITED PARTNERSHIPS

A family limited partnership (FLP) operates very much like other limited partnerships except that ownership of the partnership units is restricted to family members. The general partners control the operations and make day-to-day investment decisions, while the limited partners have ownership interests but only limited control.

In recent years, FLPs have become extremely popular for estate planning and asset protection. An FLP allows you to dispose of assets for estate tax purposes, yet retain control over those assets.

Keeping the Reins

To see how an FLP might work, consider the case of Dick and Diane Smith. They are in their mid-60s, with two children, George and Gloria.

Dick and Diane create an FLP and transfer stocks, bonds, mutual funds, investment property, and shares in a family business into it. They retain a 1% general partnership and transfer the 99% limited partnership interest to their children.

Thus, 99% of the assets (and any subsequent appreciation) won't be included in the parents' taxable estate. Yet as general partners they still make all the management decisions regarding the business, the real estate, the securities, and so forth. The FLP may even pay Dick and Diane a management fee.

There may be asset protection advantages, too. Someone who sues Dick and receives an award for damages may not be able to collect from the FLP's assets. Depending on the circumstances, a creditor's redress might be limited to a "charging order," meaning that the creditor won't collect until the FLP makes distributions to the limited partners—and that decision is in the hands of Dick and Diane, the general partners.

Trimming Transfer Taxes

Enhancing these advantages, the IRS has conceded that valuation discounts may be appropriate for transfers of illiquid, minority interests in certain assets.

Suppose that Dick and Diane own 100% of a business valued at $1 million. If they give 20% of the shares to their kids, that gift probably should not be valued at $200,000 because an independent buyer is not likely to pay that much for a 20% share in a family company. A discount of, say, 25% ($50,000) might be claimed, valuing the transfer at $150,000.

An FLP may help to increase the size of such valuation discounts. In this example, if George and Gloria received gifts of shares outright they could sell them to a willing buyer at a given price.

On the other hand, if they received FLP interests and the shares were held inside the partnership, George and Gloria might not be able to transfer their interests without the general partners' consent. Even if that consent was available, a buyer probably would be less interested in acquiring limited partnership interests than in buying the shares outright.

The bottom line: An FLP might enable you to transfer $2 million worth of assets to your children while incurring a taxable gift of only $1.5 million, $1.2 million, or even $1 million. Valuation discounts may be available even on transfers of publicly traded securities.

A Dependable Defense

The IRS has indicated it will look hard at valuation discounts claimed by FLPs. Indeed, 14% of all gift and estate tax returns under examination involve FLPs, the *Wall Street Journal* has reported.

Therefore, all the formalities should be followed closely. A genuine partnership must be formed and there should be a separate bank account for the partnership along with correspondence among the partners referring to the partnership's existence.

In addition, there should be other reasons for forming an FLP besides tax avoidance. Those reasons should be set out in the partnership agreement.

Possible reasons for creating an FLP might include:

- ✔ Asset protection
- ✔ Centralized management of investment real estate
- ✔ A desire to keep a portfolio of marketable securities intact
- ✔ Volume discounts on portfolio management fees
- ✔ Aid for family members who are incapable of managing their own assets
- ✔ Avoidance of conflicts among family members
- ✔ Education of younger family members about wealth management

IRREVOCABLE DYNASTY TRUSTS

dynasty trust
a trust designed to hold assets for the benefit of the creator's descendants.

Irrevocable *dynasty trusts*, once created, cannot be revoked! These independent entities can be funded, free of gift and estate taxes, via the unified credit, the $10,000 annual gift tax exclusion, and the generation-skipping transfer tax exemption.

The trust creator funds the trust and designates a trustee to control the trust assets. Typically, the creator's children and grandchildren are beneficiaries of this type of trust. If drafted correctly, one or more of the beneficiaries can also fill the role of trustee.

Irrevocable dynasty trusts are designed to remove assets (and their appreciation) from the creator's taxable estate, and from the reach of creditors. If implemented properly, trust assets will also stay outside of the children's taxable estates with ultimate distribution made to the grandchildren, or in some circumstances, even the great-grandchildren, completely free of estate taxes.

Chapter 14

The Wondrous
Wealth Trust

The previous chapter covered the basics of estate taxes and estate planning. How can you avoid punishing estate taxes and maximize what you'll leave to your descendants? The Wealth Trust® can accomplish these goals while providing an ideal environment for investments to grow.

The Wealth Trust is a nationally trademarked irrevocable dynasty trust utilized by Wealth Transfer Planning, Inc. This trust was designed to offer today's estate owner many of the tremendous benefits enjoyed by some of America's wealthiest families, who have refined the use of irrevocable dynasty trusts.

The Wealth Trust is a living trust. It is created while you (the *trust grantor*) are alive rather than at your death.

It is an irrevocable trust, so it can't be canceled or materially altered. (Trusts become irrevocable when you sign the documents; before that, you set the terms and conditions of the trust. So a Wealth Trust is a reflection of your goals and plans.)

The Wealth Trust is an *asset protection trust*. You can't transfer assets to cheat known creditors, but you can transfer assets out of the reach of future creditors, claimants, divorcing in-laws, and so on. This capability

trust grantor
the person who creates and funds a trust.

asset protection trust
a trust designed to preserve the assets from future creditors' claims.

makes the trust an effective tool for reducing estate taxes. Once assets are beyond the reach of your creditors, they're considered to be outside of your taxable estate as well.

As a dynasty trust it can cover your lifetime as well as those of your children and grandchildren. If you wish, the trust won't terminate until the last of your grandchildren dies and then the assets will be distributed to your great-grandchildren. Of course, you can structure a Wealth Trust that will end sooner.

These are growth trusts. Assets transferred into them can be invested and may accumulate earnings over the long term.

A Wealth Trust can be a taxpayer. In some circumstances, income may be taxed to the trust at lower rates than would be paid by you or your family members.

Normally, the money in the trust should be the last money you ever use. However, if unforeseen events arise, the trust can serve as an emergency retirement plan. Assets may be distributed to close family members during your lifetime or even, in some circumstances, to you, the trust grantor.

If properly established, the trust can serve as a landlord. It can own one or more real estate properties for use by the trust beneficiaries at little or no cost.

The trust can serve as a banker. The trustee can be given the power to lend money to the beneficiaries for certain purposes, such as starting a business.

If one of your family members has special needs, the trustee can see to that beneficiary's well-being. At the same time, the trust can alleviate family concerns such as protecting vulnerable family members from predators and even from their own weaknesses.

probate
the process of proving a will, which may be expensive and time-consuming.

The trust avoids *probate*. Assets owned by the trust won't go through probate at the death of you or your spouse. It provides privacy. While your will must be open to the public, provisions in trust documents are not exposed to prying eyes.

A trust provides seamless continuity in case of incapacity. Unfortunately, many of us will reach a point where we no longer can manage our own affairs. Assets held in trust will be managed by a trustee or a successor no matter what happens to the grantor's mental or physical well-being.

TWO VERSIONS OF THE WEALTH TRUST

A *joint donor Wealth Trust* (the type that's usually created) is funded with gifts from a married couple. In 1999, a married couple can give away up to $1.3 million without owing gift tax. That number will gradually increase to $2 million by the year 2006.

> **joint donor Wealth Trust**
> a Wealth Trust funded by assets transferred from two spouses.

You also can fund a Wealth Trust by using the annual gift tax exclusion, which will not count against the gift tax limits mentioned. A married couple can give as much as $20,000 per year per trust beneficiary and maintain a gift tax exclusion. In one court case, gift tax exclusions were upheld for a trust with 18 beneficiaries!

A *personal access version Wealth Trust* is funded by gifts from one spouse. Indeed, each spouse can have his or her own Wealth Trust. If one spouse creates the trust (becomes the grantor), the initial tax-free funding can be only half as much. However, the other spouse may serve as trustee and make distributions to the trust beneficiaries, including himself or herself.

> **personal access version Wealth Trust**
> a Wealth Trust funded by only one spouse, who may name the other spouse as trustee and beneficiary.

IN CASE OF EMERGENCY . . .

To see how the Wealth Trust can serve as an emergency retirement plan, consider the example of John Smith, a successful business owner. John transferred some of his wealth to his wife Mary, who used $650,000 to fund a personal access version of the Wealth Trust, naming John as trustee. Their children and grandchildren are named as beneficiaries, along with John.

John, as trustee, can distribute trust assets to any of the beneficiaries, including himself. If such distributions are required by the trust documents to be for health, education, maintenance, or support, the trust assets will not be included in John's taxable estate. In practice, virtually any important need can be covered by those four words, so John can distribute funds to himself if they're needed.

FAIR BUT FIRM

You can serve as the trustee of your spouse's personal access version of the Wealth Trust. However, if you're the grantor you should not be the trustee, too, because the IRS and creditors may assert that trust assets really belong to you.

In many cases, you would name a child as trustee or your children as cotrustees. Your grandchildren can be designated as successor trustees, after your children no longer are able to serve.

Another approach is to name a close family friend, a personal adviser, or a relative (a cousin, perhaps) as trustee. Such trustees need to be paid, but they may be able to arbitrate family disputes. Your first concern should be to name a friendly trustee who will be sympathetic to the needs of the trust beneficiaries.

Normally, the trustee should be able to distribute trust income (and principal, in some circumstances) to the trust beneficiaries, at the trustee's discretion.

VITAL INGREDIENTS

To make a regular irrevocable trust into a Wealth Trust, two powers should be added:

First, include a provision enabling the trustee to buy and hold residential real estate. The trustee should be given the discretionary power—but not the obligation—to let the beneficiaries use the trust property or properties.

Second, add a provision enabling the trustee, with the consent of the beneficiaries, to make distributions to pay the premiums for life insurance covering your grandchildren, which might come in handy if your grandchildren leave taxable estates. Assuming your grandchildren are very young when the policies are purchased, such insurance will be relatively inexpensive.

In most cases, your children and grandchildren will be the beneficiaries. Working with a savvy attorney, you can get yet-unborn descendants added to the list.

GRANDCHILDREN'S INCENTIVE TRUST

If your main goal is simply to keep your own estate intact, your Wealth Trust can terminate after you and your spouse die. Alternatively, it can remain intact throughout your grandchildren's lives.

If you name your grandchildren as beneficiaries, you might want to consider a special version of the Wealth Trust, the *Grandchildren's Incentive Trust.*® All present and future grandchildren may automatically be included as beneficiaries.

Upon your death, the trust splits into a separate trust for each grandchild. Typically, your children will be the trustees of each trust until each grandchild reaches a specified age (such as 35) and succeeds as trustee.

What are the advantages of the Grandchildren's Incentive Trust? Such a trust can:

> **Grandchildren's Incentive Trust**
> a trust with provisions designed to motivate young beneficiaries to behave in a certain manner.

✔ Provide funds for college and postgraduate education

✔ Motivate your grandchildren to expand their personal earnings

✔ Provide seed capital for business start-ups and other opportunities

✔ Pay for wedding and honeymoon expenses

✔ Make a down payment on a first home purchase

✔ Act as a personal, friendly banker when needed

✔ Pay for medical expenses and other emergencies

✔ Help your grandchildren's children: your great-grandchildren

Moreover, the Grandchildren's Incentive Trust can be structured to provide an incentive for your grandchildren to succeed in their own careers. You can specify that the trustee will distribute to each grandchild a certain per-centage (10% to 50%) of that grandchild's earnings each year.

The bottom line is that your grandchildren will en-joy financial security and the ability to take advantage of opportunities but won't be spoiled by a large inheritance. What better gift can a proud grandparent provide?

FUNDING YOUR TRUST

Normally, a trust of this type is funded with cash. How-ever, other assets (securities, real estate, business inter-ests) may be transferred into the trust. For estate planning purposes, you should give away assets likely to appreciate because all appreciation after the date of transfer will be out of your taxable estate.

If you give away assets that are difficult to value, such as real estate and interests in a closely held business, you should have an unrelated party perform an appraisal at the time of transfer.

Another noncash asset that may be hard to value is a cash value life insurance policy. If you want to transfer such a policy to a trust, ask the company or your insur-ance agent for a valuation. Such a policy must be trans-ferred at least three years before your death in order to be excluded from your estate.

INVESTING TRUST ASSETS

If you fund a trust with cash, the trustee will have to invest the funds. You can discuss the use of trust funds with the trustee but you can't compel obedience to your wishes.

Often, life insurance is held inside a trust. Such poli-cies might cover your life, the lives of you and your spouse, or your descendants. With life insurance, you know that a substantial amount will be paid to the trust when someone dies.

Money invested in cash value life insurance won't be taxed as it compounds. In fact, the trustee may be able to borrow against the policy, tax-free, and distribute cash to investors.

When the insured individual or individuals die, the trust collects the proceeds tax-free. What's more, when a trust is fully invested in life insurance, there is no need to report income to the IRS each year.

Other investment alternatives may exist, especially if you're in poor health so the trust will have to pay very large sums to insure your life. The trustee might invest in municipal bonds for tax-exempt interest, growth stocks that are lightly taxed because they pay low dividends, or a combination of stocks, bonds, and life insurance.

LIFE INSURANCE ADVANTAGES

There are two benefits to using life insurance to fund your trust: Your loved ones will be protected in case of your untimely death, and death benefits will likely be tax-free.

For example, Al Brown and Carl Dean both decide to fund a trust. Al's trust is funded by growth stocks. Each year he transfers $50,000 to the trust, which the trustee invests in the stock market.

After three years and $150,000 worth of investments, the trust might own a portfolio worth $200,000, including appreciation. However, if Al dies then, the trust will have only $200,000 to provide for his loved ones.

On the other hand, Carl decides to use life insurance to fund his trust. He, too, transfers $50,000 per year to the trust, which the trustee uses to pay premiums on a $2 million policy. If Carl dies after three years, the trust will receive $2 million in death benefits.

In this example, Al's trust won't even have $200,000 to distribute. The trustee will have to sell shares in order to raise cash for distributions, and each sale of appreciated stock will trigger a capital gains tax.

Assume a 25% capital gains tax rate, including state and federal tax. Al has a $50,000 capital gain (he invested $150,000 and the stocks are now worth $200,000), so $12,500 in tax would be due. The assets in the trust really are worth only $187,500, after-tax.

By contrast, life insurance death benefits aren't subject to income tax, in most cases. Therefore, the trust that Carl funds with life insurance will have a full $2 million, after-tax. That's why life insurance is a popular choice for funding a trust.

Think of the money in your trust as the last money you'll want to use. You and your family will prefer to maximize the tax-favored growth. However, in case of an emergency, the trustee can distribute funds to the trust beneficiaries, who are also family members. No other strategy is nearly as powerful when it comes to providing long-term security for your loved ones.

Chapter

Super Estate-Tax Reduction Strategies

As mentioned earlier, you can give away $10,000 per recipient per year with no gift tax consequences. (Married couples can give away $20,000 per recipient per year.) In addition, there's a lifetime exemption for gift and estate taxes that will rise from $675,000 in 2000 to $1 million in 2006.

Families with larger estates, though, will have to pay gift or estate taxes, or both, on asset transfers. You might invest wisely all your life, building up a portfolio worth several million dollars, only to bequeath to your heirs a seven-figure estate tax bill.

This chapter illustrates some advanced techniques for reducing such taxes.

A COLD SHOULDER FOR THE TAX COLLECTOR

If you use a unique *super-freeze* technique, you can sell assets within your family with minimal costs and tax consequences. To see how a super-freeze might work, consider the example of Bob and Sue Davis, who are in their mid-70s with four children and five grandchildren.

> **APRIL**
> **15**
> **super-freeze**
> a sophisticated estate planning strategy designed to remove future asset appreciation from someone's estate.

Not only do they want to minimize estate taxes, they are extremely interested in privacy and keeping their holdings confidential.

By 1999, Bob and Sue had utilized their $1.3 million-per-couple unified credit transfer allowance by giving assets to their children. In addition, they had been giving $20,000 per year to each of their children and grandchildren.

For further tax relief, Bob and Sue implemented the super-freeze strategy. Here's how it worked:

First, they established a family limited partnership (FLP) and placed $1 million worth of assets on the general partnership side. Bob named himself the general partner, in control of the FLP.

Then they placed $10 million worth of assets on the limited partnership side, with Bob and Sue as the limited partners. Up to this point, no taxes were due.

The next step was to establish a grantor trust—a trust where the grantor is responsible for the income taxes but the trust assets are out of the grantor's taxable estate.

Then the trust purchased the limited partnership side of the partnership, which held $10 million of securities. This purchase was structured using an interest-bearing *balloon payment note*. In order for such a sale to be recognized, the trust must be a "trust of substance."

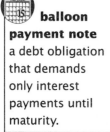

balloon payment note
a debt obligation that demands only interest payments until maturity.

SHREWD GIVING

To make the trust a trust of substance, Bob and Sue gave $500,000 in cash to the trust, incurring a $200,000 gift tax. In addition, they made sure that the generation-skipping provisions were met by subtracting the $500,000 gift from the $2 million generation-skipping tax (GST) exemption that each married couple has. With the $500,000, the trust purchased $7 million worth of *second-to-die life insurance* on Bob and Sue.

Now, the trust had substance so it was able to purchase the $10 million limited partnership interest. Because a limited partnership is controlled by the general

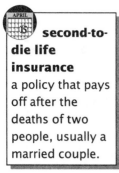

second-to-die life insurance
a policy that pays off after the deaths of two people, usually a married couple.

partner, the assets were discounted by 30%, resulting in a $7 million purchase price.

Thus, for a $7 million note the trust was able to purchase the limited partnership interest that held $10 million (face value) worth of assets.

What's more, the $7 million note effectively held by Bob and Sue is frozen: It will never increase in value even if the $10 million worth of assets in the trust appreciates.

As a result, Bob and Sue have removed $3 million worth of assets from their estate. Should Bob or Sue live long enough for the $10 million of assets to double to $20 million, they will have removed $13 million from their estate, for a $200,000 gift tax payment.

What's more, the trust now holds $7 million worth of insurance on Bob and Sue's lives. After Bob and Sue die, the $7 million of life insurance will pay off the $7 million note.

In the meanwhile, Bob, as the general partner, will sell off enough assets each year to pay the interest on the note, after paying capital gains tax. Because the trust is a grantor trust, the income may be taxable to Bob and Sue as a long-term capital gain, taxed at 20% (perhaps 18% in the future). If the income had been taxable to the trust, the tax rate would be 39.6%.

The trust that holds this growing portfolio can stay in existence for three generations in the state where Bob and Sue live. Later, it can be transferred to a state that permits perpetual trusts so it can last as long as future beneficiaries wish.

Thus, the millions of dollars in the trust can stay in the family for at least 100 years and maybe for up to 1,000 years. The trust can subdivide in the future, for easier management. The net result is that Bob and Sue have cut millions from their estate tax bill and arranged their affairs so that those millions benefit their descendants for generations to come.

PROTECTED RETIREMENT ACCOUNT

The *protected retirement account* strategy combines retirement planning and estate planning goals to provide both

protected retirement account
a strategy that calls for a trust to buy a cash-value life insurance policy that can be tapped for tax-free retirement income.

you and your heirs with significant tax benefits and asset protection. The protected retirement account is a marriage of the personal access version of the Wealth Trust and a cash-rich life insurance–based private pension plan. Here are the key points:

✔ First, a trust is established by a single creator, who names a spouse as the trustee.

✔ Second, the donor-spouse transfers funds from separately owned property to the trust for a 7- to 10-year period.

✔ Third, the trust purchases a cash-rich life insurance policy on the life of the donor-spouse.

Current tax law allows income to be withdrawn from this specially constructed life insurance policy 100% income-tax-free. This means that the beneficiaries of the trust, via the trustee, can receive tax-free retirement income in the form of withdrawals from the cash values of the policy. The fact that the insurance is owned by the personal access version of the Wealth Trust also adds an element of creditor protection.

BUSINESS SUCCESSION PLANNING

buy-sell agreement
a contract spelling out the terms of business succession in case of death, retirement, or disability.

The survival of a family business upon its transfer to a new generation depends largely on the effectiveness of the succession plan implemented by the transferor. Ideally, that plan will minimize transfer taxes, assure sufficient liquidity, provide for an orderly transition of control over management of the business, and safeguard the interests of both participating and nonparticipating family members. Once finalized, that plan can be memorialized in a *buy-sell agreement*.

One of the most important functions of a buy-sell agreement is to provide the decedent's estate with liquidity with which to pay estate taxes or support the family in the event of death or disability while protecting the integrity of the business in the event that the business owner and spouse divorce.

Without proper funding to achieve the necessary liquidity, the most carefully drafted buy-sell agreement is useless. Although several funding methods can be used, the purchase of life insurance is probably the most common, most efficient, and least expensive method of funding a buy-sell agreement. Life insurance is the only funding method available that guarantees that the necessary dollars will be available exactly when needed.

The highest and best use of life insurance to fund a buyout lies in structuring its purchase to minimize the income and estate consequences to the persons or entities participating in the agreement. One insurance option that may achieve this goal is split dollar life insurance (see Chapter 11).

PENSION PHILANTHROPY

During your lifetime you are likely to benefit significantly from the tax deferral enjoyed by your retirement plan. However, the double tax burden of income and estate taxes imposed on retirement assets transferred at death will substantially deplete what the next generation receives.

Therefore, if you have a sizable retirement plan you should consider making charitable entities your plan beneficiaries. Moreover, by utilizing a charitable remainder trust (CRT) you can name your heirs (probably your children) as the income beneficiaries, thus potentially increasing the net amount received by both your heirs and your favorite charities.

In the following example, Dr. Smith is an 80-year-old widower and owner of a $2 million IRA, with a total estate of $5 million. He has two children, aged 50 and 46, who are in the highest federal income tax bracket.

If Dr. Smith dies in 2000 and has named his children as his IRA beneficiaries, his beneficiaries are likely to net about $2.4 million, after estate tax and income tax on his IRA. On the other hand, if Dr. Smith had named a CRT as his IRA beneficiary and designated his children as the CRT income beneficiaries, the $2 million in the IRA would go to the CRT.

Assuming that Dr. Smith's children receive a 6% payout from the CRT, based on their joint life expectancy they should receive annual income of $120,000 for approximately 35 years, for a total of $4.2 million. If invested with a return of 6%, they should also receive annual income from the balance of the estate of approximately $50,000. Thus, their total annual income stream should equal some $170,000. After the children's deaths (assuming annual growth of 6%), charity should receive approximately $2 million.

If Dr. Smith's children simply received $2.4 million outright (without the use of a CRT), they would enjoy an annual income stream of about $145,000 (with a return of 6%). But by including a charitable entity in his plan, Dr. Smith will pass an additional $25,000 in annual income to his children while also giving a generous $2 million to his favorite charity.

PHILANTHROPIC POWER PLAY

A CRT, a Wealth Trust, and a private family foundation can be combined to yield the ultimate philanthropic power play. For example:

Sam Carter and his wife Susan are both 60 years of age, with an estate worth approximately $5 million. They have three children. Sam and Susan own a large block of publicly traded stock, currently valued at $2 million, which they accumulated as part of Sam's company's bonus plan. Their cost basis is $500,000.

If Sam and Susan wish to sell their stock, they will pay $300,000 in capital gains taxes (assuming a 20% tax bracket), leaving $1.7 million for future investments. If they decide not to sell, their children could owe $1.1 million in estate taxes (assuming a 55% estate tax rate) and be left with a $900,000 inheritance.

Instead, Sam and Susan create a CRT, to which they donate the $2 million worth of stock. Acting as trustee, Sam sells the stock; because the trust is tax-exempt, no capital gains tax need be paid. Sam then reinvests the $2 million in mutual funds and realizes a 10% total rate of return.

Sam and Susan elect to receive an 8% payout from the CRT, which will generate an income of $160,000 per year (approximately $102,400 after taxes, assuming a 36% income tax rate). As the trust assets increase in value, their income will increase proportionately. Sam and Susan also receive an income tax deduction, based on the present value of the charitable remainder interest, of approximately $82,000.

After Sam and Susan die, the $2 million in the CRT will go to the Sam and Susan Carter Family Foundation. As required by law, the family foundation's 5% charitable distribution obligation will be $100,000 per year. The foundation can use the remaining $100,000 per year (assuming a 10% return) to pay its expenses, including salaries to the directors (Sam and Susan's children).

In order to replace their children's inheritance, which is lost through creation of the CRT and private family foundation, Sam and Susan establish a Wealth Trust, naming their children as trustees and funding it with 10 annual gifts of $36,000. The children, as trustees, buy $1.5 million worth of second-to-die insurance for a premium of approximately $36,000 per year over a 10-year period (given current interest rate assumptions).

If Sam and Susan each live to age 80, they will have received after-tax income from their CRT of approximately $2.5 million (assuming a 10% return on the mutual funds held by the CRT). They will have also made a $2 million donation to their family foundation that will greatly benefit their favorite charities.

Moreover, when Sam and Susan die, their children will receive $1.5 million in life insurance benefits, tax-free. The children will also receive continuing income as directors of the family foundation.

LEVERAGING YOUR LEGACY

Combining a charitable lead trust (CLT) with a private foundation can enable you to reap tremendous estate and generation-skipping transfer tax savings while also making a significant philanthropic contribution. This strategic

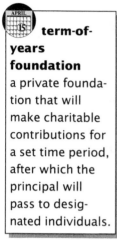

term-of-years foundation
a private foundation that will make charitable contributions for a set time period, after which the principal will pass to designated individuals.

combination, known as the *term-of-years foundation*, allows you to leverage your unified credit and generation-skipping transfer tax exemption on gifts to your grandchildren. This leverage occurs because estate tax liability is calculated based on the present value of a future gift—the grandchildren do not receive the gift until the "term of years" (the period during which a private foundation enjoys use of the assets) has expired.

Suppose, for example, Emily Smith leaves her $5 million estate to her grandchildren via her will; after the unified credit her family will face an estate tax liability of approximately $2.2 million.

Moreover, usage of her entire $1 million generation-skipping transfer tax exemption would leave a generation-skipping transfer tax of approximately $1 million. Therefore, out of a $5 million bequest the grandchildren would receive less than $2 million.

On the other hand, Emily could leave $5 million to a CLT for a term of 25 years, with the remainder to her grandchildren. Based on several assumptions (including a 7% payout to the charitable beneficiary and anticipated growth of the assets at 7% per year), the present value of the remainder interest (the present value of what is left to the grandchildren) would be valued at approximately $950,000. After full utilization of the donor's $675,000 unified credit allocation, estate taxes would be less than $100,000.

Further, usage of Emily's $1 million generation-skipping transfer tax exemption would result in the imposition of no generation-skipping transfer taxes. At the end of the term of years, more than $4.9 million would transfer to the grandchildren, free of taxes.

Thus, in this example, Emily Smith can effectively leverage her unified credit and generation-skipping transfer tax exemption to shelter almost $5 million from taxes.

Even better, rather than allowing the federal government to take about $3.2 million from her estate (in the form of estate and generation-skipping transfer taxes, as in the direct bequest example) she can instead leave roughly $8.75 million (7% × $5 million = $350,000 × 25 years = $8.75 million) to worthwhile charities!

REAL ANSWERS FOR REAL ESTATE

An ideal succession plan for property owners will minimize transfer taxes, assure sufficient liquidity, provide for an orderly transition of control over management of the properties, and safeguard the interests of both participating and nonparticipating family members. Combining a well-drafted, well-thought-out plan with an FLP, a Wealth Trust, and survivorship life insurance should allow you to reach these necessary goals.

For example, Mike and Mary Evans own several residential rental properties that they manage themselves. Currently, these properties are valued at nearly $4 million. Mike and Mary (both aged 55) would like their four children to have the opportunity to own and operate these properties one day. However, they face two problems.

Their first problem is estate taxes. Even assuming that proper planning shelters $2 million from estate taxes after 2006, and assuming no growth on the value of the rental properties, after Mike and Mary die their children will owe federal estate taxes of approximately $1 million.

Their second problem is that the children will have no liquidity with which to pay the taxes. Thus, they may be forced to liquidate some or even all of the properties to come up with the necessary cash.

Fortunately, they can plan solutions for these problems.

First, Mike and Mary can establish an FLP and transfer their rental properties to the partnership. They will divide the partnership into a 1% general partner interest and a 99% limited partnership interest. Initially they will own both the general and limited interests.

Next, Mike and Mary can give 49.5% of the limited shares to a Wealth Trust established for the benefit of their children and even their future grandchildren. Moreover, they can make this gift to the trust without paying gift tax by allocating their unified credits.

Ordinarily, the unified credit can shelter up to $1.35 million in 2000 (increasing to $2 million by 2006) per couple from estate and gift taxes. However, discounts on the value of the transferred limited partnership shares should be available, due to the lack of control and lack of marketability inherent in limited partnership interests.

Therefore (assuming application of a 35% discount, as calculated by an independent appraisal firm), Mike and Mary can gift limited partnership units with a value of $1.3 million that represent underlying assets with a value of approximately $2 million. This gifting should not trigger a tax.

One or more of the Evans children can act as trustee of the Wealth Trust. The trustee(s) can use cash flow generated by the 49.5% limited partnership interest to fund purchase of a survivorship life insurance policy on Mike's and Mary's lives. Premiums of approximately $20,500 per year for 11 years should support a death benefit of $1 million. After Mike and Mary have died, the $1 million will be available to provide the children with liquidity necessary to keep the real estate assets intact.

Chapter

Last Lessons
in Tax Savings

Educating your children can be devastatingly expensive. Fortunately, tax relief exists.

✔ Income-producing investments can be placed in your child's name. Children aged 14 and older are taxed at their own rate, so they will pay less in tax.

Unfortunately, children under age 14 are basically taxed at your rate. Nonetheless, even this age group enjoys a minor tax break. Their first $700 (in 2000) in unearned income is tax-free, and the next $700 (up to a total of $1,400) is taxed at the child's rate (typically 15%). Unearned income over $1,400 is taxed at the parents' rate, called the *kiddie tax*.

✔ Funds can be gifted to your child (in most states) through the Uniform Gifts to Minors Act (UGMA) or Uniform Transfer to Minors Act (UTMA). These acts authorize *custodial accounts* for minors, which can easily be set up by banks, brokers, mutual funds, and so forth. The custodian (you) oversees the growth of the account, while taking advantage of the beneficiary's (your child's) more favorable tax bracket. When your child reaches age 21 (18 in some states), the funds are turned over to him or her.

Caution: If you fund a UGMA or UTMA account, the

kiddie tax
the tax code provision that treats some unearned income of children under 14 as being earned by their parents.

custodial account
an arrangement that permits minors to hold assets, which will become their property when they come of age.

account balance may be included in your taxable estate if you die while serving as custodian. Further, a grandparent who donates to such an account may trigger generation-skipping transfer tax implications.

✔ Unique opportunities may be available if U.S. savings bonds, purchased in the parents' names, are used to pay for a child's college tuition (see Chapter 3).

The largest benefits can be reaped if saving begins early. The sooner you begin saving, the longer you can benefit from the magic of compound earnings and the larger the nest egg you will have available when your child is ready to pursue advanced education.

FEDS TO THE RESCUE

APRIL 15 **qualified state tuition plan**
program that provides tax deferral and tax-bracket reduction to encourage investing for higher education.

Under a federal law passed in 1996 and amended in 1997, *qualified state tuition plans* offer tax benefits to everyone, regardless of income. Most states offer such plans and many of them add their own state tax benefits as well.

Although each state's plan is unique, there are some common features:

- ✔ You open an account by investing certain amounts, up to $100,000 in states such as Indiana and New Hampshire.

- ✔ You can invest a lump sum or make a series of payments.

- ✔ The money that you contribute is invested on your behalf and any earnings are tax-deferred. That is, your investment will compound with no reduction for income tax.

- ✔ The money in the plan can be used for college tuition, fees, room, board, and books.

- ✔ When the money comes out of the plan to pay such expenses, it will be taxed on a FIFO (first in, first out) basis.

Suppose, for example, you invest $100,000 and it grows to $180,000 by the time your child starts college. The first $100,000 to come out of the fund won't be taxed as long as the money is used for qualified expenses; the remaining $80,000 will continue to build up, tax-deferred. Only after all of your contributions are withdrawn will any tax be due on withdrawals of earnings.

Further suppose, in the third year of your child's college career, the $100,000 that you contributed to the account has all been spent and another $20,000 is pulled from the plan to cover college bills. That year, $20,000 worth of income will have to be recognized.

This income will be reported on your child's tax return and probably taxed at 15%. Thus, these plans offer tax reduction as well as deferral.

As mentioned, state tax breaks also may be available. New York, for example, lets couples deduct up to $10,000 in annual contributions, while Iowa allows contributors to deduct $2,000 per year per child from state income taxes.

Most states won't impose state taxes on the earnings when they're withdrawn, as long as the money is used to pay college bills in-state. (Some states offer further financial incentives, such as matching contributions.)

THE GIVING IS GOOD

Besides the federal and state income tax consequences described in the prior section, federal gift taxes need to be considered. Contributions to such plans are considered gifts but they count toward the $10,000 annual gift tax exclusion ($20,000 for married couples).

That is, you and your spouse are allowed to give your daughter Jill $20,000 this year, free of gift tax, but if you contribute $12,000 to a college savings plan on her behalf your remaining gift tax exclusion for Jill in this year will be reduced to $8,000. If you (or perhaps a doting grandparent) make a larger donation—up to $50,000—to a state tuition plan, the donor can elect to spread the outlay over five years for gift tax purposes.

As this indicates, you're not the only one who can contribute to your child's account: Friends and relatives also may make contributions. Indeed, such a plan may be ideal for periodic birthday and holiday gifts. Why put Uncle John's $50 check into the bank, where interest is taxable, when it could go directly into a tax-sheltered state tuition plan?

BEYOND TAXES

With these plans the money belongs to the parent, not the child, if the child decides against going to college. Therefore, such college savings plans may be better than custodial accounts for college savings.

Why? If you use custodial accounts, the money belongs to the child upon coming of age, often at 18. With custodial accounts parents run the risk their kids will take the money and run off, rather than go to college, but that won't be possible with the money in a qualified state tuition plan.

These plans vary widely from state to state. Several plans permit out-of-state residents to invest. In many cases, the money that's saved can be used for out-of-state as well as in-state college expenses.

Although all of these plans invest the money that's contributed, there are great differences in how they invest. The first state tuition plans paid a guaranteed rate that was pegged to some measure of college inflation. That was attractive 15 or 20 years ago, when college costs were rising at a double-digit pace, but recent increases in expenses have averaged only 4% to 5% per year, so plans that promise such returns may seem unappealing.

Newer state tuition plans tend to turn the money over to investment professionals who'll invest the portfolio in a mix of stocks and bonds. In such plans, the amount of the tax-deferred buildup will depend on the success of the manager making the investments.

A key factor, then, is the investment philosophy of the plan. Some states give youngsters under age 6 a 90% allocation to stocks, shifting to 90% in bonds by age 17.

In some states 55% of a newborn's portfolio is placed in stocks and that portion falls to 10% for 16-year-olds. Taking a less aggressive posture, some states limit stocks to no more than 40% while still other states avoid stocks altogether.

CONTROL FACTORS

In any state plan, though, you're giving up control over that part of your portfolio. If you are willing to take responsibility for your portfolio, you may do as well or better investing on your own.

What about the tax benefits you'll sacrifice by not investing through these state tuition plans? An alternative college funding plan needn't be too taxing.

If you invest in growth stocks and stock funds and refrain from active trading, you probably won't incur a large tax bill each year. Then, when you sell, you'll owe tax on any gains at only 20%. What's more, if you give the appreciated shares to your kids when it's time to pay college bills, they can sell the shares and likely owe tax at a 10% rate.

In addition to variations in investment policies, state plans differ in other respects. There are varying rules on the amount you're permitted to invest, the treatment of accounts used for out-of-state education, and guaranteed returns.

Plans also diverge in the way they handle installment payments. Your contract may be subject to cancellation if you don't maintain the promised payments, and there may be no refunds until the scheduled payout date unless your child dies or becomes disabled.

Another point you need to consider: What if your child doesn't go to college—or if your youngster wins a scholarship and doesn't need the money? Typically, you can transfer the account to the name of another child. If no one will use the account for college, you'll get your money back, perhaps after suffering a penalty that reduces the earnings you'll receive.

The bottom line is that qualified state tuition plans

are an option to consider—especially the plan offered in your home state—but you should learn all the details before investing. To keep up on plans across the nation, check out the web site run by the College Plan Savings Network (www.collegesavings.org).

DOUBLE JEOPARDY: THE AMT

alternative minimum tax (AMT)
a parallel tax system. Taxpayers pay whichever is higher, the regular tax or the AMT.

Periodically, the media report that a certain number of Americans earn zillions of dollars yet pay pennies in income tax. To rein in such atrocities, Congress created the *alternative minimum tax (AMT)*.

As is sometimes the case, a rifle shot from Washington winds up as buckshot by the time it reaches the target: Now, you don't have to be rich to be ensnared by the AMT. The AMT increasingly affects people of moderate incomes who live in high-tax states and cities. The higher your total deductions, as a percentage of income, the greater the likelihood you'll be exposed to the AMT. If you fall victim to the AMT, your tax bill is heading north—and some of your after-tax investment returns may go south.

Trapping the Not-So-Rich

The Congressional Joint Committee on Taxation estimates that the number of taxpayers paying the AMT reached 856,000 in 1998, more than double the number in 1995. Moreover, the current number is expected to increase more than tenfold by 2008, to 8.8 million taxpayers. Reportedly, families with incomes as low as $60,000 will be vulnerable by then.

The reason? The AMT is not indexed to inflation, while the regular tax system is. Thus, taxes owed under the AMT are going up faster than regular income tax. Originally designed to catch people who overloaded on tax shelters, the AMT now traps those with large amounts of state and local taxes, home equity interest, stock options, and so on.

A Lose-Lose Scenario

You may be able to avoid or minimize the AMT with careful planning. First, however, you need to understand how it works. In essence, the AMT is an income tax that's calculated in a different manner than the regular income tax. Each year, taxpayers are supposed to calculate their tax obligation both ways and pay whichever tax bill turns out to be higher, the AMT or the regular tax.

Thus, if Larry Jones owes $60,000 on his AMT and $70,000 on his regular tax, he pays his regular income tax. But if Linda Smith owes $80,000 on her regular tax and $90,000 on her AMT, she pays her AMT. The IRS always wins in this game.

Period of Adjustments

Why are the totals different in the two tax systems? The AMT calculation starts with regular taxable income, which is increased by certain *AMT adjustments*. Fewer itemized deductions are allowed for AMT purposes, no deduction is allowed for personal exemptions, and a number of tax preference items are also added back to taxable income.

> **AMT adjustments** tax benefits that are added back to income when calculating an AMT obligation.

Thus, AMT income may be much greater than your regular taxable income. Joint filers pay 26% on $175,000 to $210,000 of AMT income and 28% on greater amounts; single filers also pay 26% and 28%, with a lower range of step-up points. AMT tax rates are lower than regular tax rates, which go up to 39.6%, but they're levied on larger amounts of income.

Creeps and Bounds

The AMT is projected to spread in future years because of a quirk in the tax code. The main factor causing "AMT creep" is that income levels and exemptions that apply under the regular tax system are indexed for inflation but the corresponding AMT brackets and exemptions are not indexed. Someone with a given level of income will see his or her regular tax gradually decrease but will not see the AMT drop.

Suppose Larry Jones has a certain level of income, which he maintains each year. Thanks to indexing, his regular tax bill will go down each year. That is, some income that was taxed at 28% will be taxed at 15%, some 31% income will be taxed at 28%, and so on.

However, while his regular income tax falls, his AMT will remain the same. At some point, the lines will cross and the AMT will exceed the regular income tax. At that point, Larry will be subject to the AMT. (If Larry's income increases, his regular tax will increase, slowing his path into AMT territory, but he'll still be moving in that direction and may get there eventually.)

Getting Hit Where You Live

The other factor that's driving up susceptibility to the AMT is the broad array of tax breaks that must be included in AMT income. State and local income taxes as well as property taxes are adjustments to income for AMT purposes. In certain high-tax areas such as New York and California, state income tax and local property tax alone can push you into the AMT. Home equity interest also may be an AMT adjustment, in some circumstances.

Suppose a married couple's regular taxable income is $150,000. If their add-back tax breaks (including state and local income and property taxes) are $34,000 or higher, they could be subject to the AMT, according to the accounting firm Ernst & Young. On a $200,000 taxable income, add-backs of $37,000 could put them over the threshold.

More Gain, More Pain

The situation is even more critical if your income consists largely of long-term capital gains. The federal tax rate on such gains is now capped at 20%, so your regular tax bill will be reduced—perhaps reduced to the point where it's below the AMT. As a greater percentage of income is comprised of long-term gains, it will take fewer preference items to trigger the AMT because the two tax calculations are lower to start with.

Suppose a couple's joint taxable income this year is $200,000 but $100,000 comes from a long-term gain. Then, if their add-backs are over $16,000 they'll have to worry about the AMT.

Stock Shock

Employees of publicly held corporations may have another AMT issue to contend with: incentive stock options (see Chapter 2). Even though no income tax is due when the options are exercised, the difference between the option price and the fair market value is an AMT adjustment at that time.

In that situation, you should consult with a tax professional to see how much you can exercise without running into the AMT. A taxpayer who exercises too many incentive stock options may owe an estimated tax penalty as well as the AMT.

Muddy Waters for Munis

Besides issues concerning incentive stock options, how does the AMT affect investors? You may owe tax on municipal bond income. Back in the 1980s, a federal tax law change created a class of *AMT munis*. That is, the interest on some "private activity" municipal bonds used to finance state and local infrastructure projects is subject to the AMT.

> **APRIL**
> **15**
>
> **AMT munis**
> tax-exempt bonds paying interest that is included in income, for AMT purposes.

In the municipal bond market, AMT munis carry higher yields than truly tax-free munis of comparable quality and maturity, which makes AMT munis extremely popular. As long as you pay regular income tax rather than the AMT, you can pocket the extra yield without having to worry. However, for taxpayers who are subject to the AMT, the interest on such bonds becomes taxable rather than tax-exempt.

Thus, investors who hold municipal bonds should start to monitor their portfolios. If you're not paying the AMT now and you hold short-term munis, there's not much to worry about. On the other hand, if you're buying long-term munis, perhaps to help pay for a child's education, you definitely should be careful about AMT bonds. That applies to zero coupon munis as well as to munis that pay current interest. Municipal bond issuers are required to disclose whether the interest is subject to the AMT, so you should read the related documents before investing.

Fund Facts

What's more, many investment pools of municipal bonds (mutual funds, closed-end funds, unit investment trusts) hold significant amounts of AMT bonds because such holdings push up their yields. If you invest in a fund with 44% AMT holdings, then 44% of the income dividends will be subject to the AMT.

Again, funds are required to disclose their holdings of AMT bonds so you need to screen such investments thoroughly before buying them and monitor them regularly thereafter. Generally, you should be particularly wary of so-called high-yield muni funds, which may hold large amounts of AMT bonds, while tax-free muni funds must keep their AMT exposure below 20%.

Credit Risk

There may be other implications for investors, too. Low-income housing partnerships (see Chapter 6), for example, deliver tax credits to investors for 10 years or longer. However, these credits can't reduce the AMT. Thus, if you invest in such a partnership you may find yourself unable to use some or even all of your tax credits in a future year.

Crunch Time

Because of all these factors, millions of moderate-income taxpayers will have to run through the incredibly complicated AMT calculations. The AMT requires thorough planning; begin by checking your tax return from last year.

A lot of people who have someone else prepare their taxes don't even realize that they've paid the AMT. The IRS won't send you a note telling you that you've paid the AMT. You can find out by looking under "Other Taxes" on the last page of your return.

If you paid the AMT last year, chances are you will again this year, unless your finances are much different now. If you didn't pay the AMT, check with your tax preparer if you have one to find out if you'll be vulnerable.

If you think you'll be in an AMT situation, reverse standard tax planning. For example, don't prepay state and local taxes in December, because those deductions won't do you any good.

If you're in a position to do so, accelerate income into the current year. As long as you're paying the AMT, you might as well increase the amount of income you receive at the relatively low rates of 26% or 28%. With a little planning, you can make the AMT your friend.

LAST WORDS: YEAR-END TAX PLANNING

Here are the things you should do every December regarding your investment portfolio to make your life less taxing the following April:

✔ Count up your realized gains and losses for the year so far. Don't forget capital gains distributions from mutual funds. (Call your funds for an idea of when you'll receive year-end distributions and how great they'll be.)

✔ For tax purposes, disregard transactions inside tax-deferred retirement plans. Only taxable transactions matter.

✔ Don't forget to include any capital loss *carryforwards* from previous years.

✔ Sell enough losers by year-end so that you wind up the year with $3,000 in net capital losses. That's the maximum amount you can deduct from the rest of your income. Of course, if you wind up with a net loss you won't owe any capital gains tax for the year.

carryforward
a tax benefit that can't be used in one year so it is deferred to a future tax return.

investment interest expense
interest paid on loans taken out to make investments.

✔ If you incurred *investment interest expense* this year (say you borrowed on margin to buy securities), check with your tax pro. You need to know whether it's best for you to wind up with capital losses, as just described, or if you should shoot for capital gains to offset your investment interest expense.

✔ If your year-end strategy calls for you to sell losers, buy a similar issue. After selling Sears, for example, buy J. C. Penney or Wal-Mart. If you are determined to include the stock you sold in your portfolio, you'll have to wait at least 31 days before buying it back.

(Another technique is to double up—buy an equivalent amount of the securities you want to sell at a loss, wait more than 30 days, then sell your original holding at a loss. However, in order to implement this technique at year-end you need to buy the new shares no later than November.)

✔ If your year-end strategy calls for you to sell winners, you can buy them back right away, if desired. You'll still have your taxable gain, to soak up realized losses, and you'll increase your basis in that stock.

✔ If you have college-bound children, give each one up to $10,000 worth of appreciated stock. (For married couples, the limit is $20,000.) Such gifts won't incur a gift tax.

You can keep the securities in a custodial account and take profits, now or in the future. As long as your children are at least 14 when the profits are taken, those profits likely will be taxed at only 10%, not the 20% you'd pay on your own gains. Then the net proceeds can be used for college bills.

flexible spending account
a fringe benefit offered by many employers. These plans permit employees to purchase goods and services with pretax rather than with after-tax dollars.

✔ Similar year-end gifts should be made to all your relatives if you're worried that you'll leave a taxable estate. The $10,000 or $20,000 annual gift tax exclusion is "use it or lose it," meaning that gifts you neglect to make one year can't be made up in the future.

✔ Use appreciated securities for year-end charitable gifts. You're giving away the tax obligation as well as the gift, yet the charity won't owe any tax when it sells the securities.

Beyond your investment portfolio, don't forget to use up any amounts left in your *flexible spending account* at work. If it's a medical account, for example, use the money left over for checkups, eyeglasses, and so forth.

The same is true if your medical expenses for the year already top 7.5% of your adjusted gross income. If this is the case, further medical outlays will be fully deductible, so you should accelerate discretionary expenses into December.

Ask your tax pro if you should prepay state and local income tax by year-end. Usually this is a good strategy. However, taxpayers are increasingly exposed to the alternative minimum tax (AMT); if you're in this category, you're better off waiting until these payments come due in January.

REALLY LAST-MINUTE TAX TIPS

After New Year's, it's still not too late to cut the tax you'll owe on your previous year's return. Here are some steps you can take:

✔ Contribute to an IRA. You can make contributions up to $2,000 per person until April 15. Under certain circumstances, those contributions will be deductible. For example, if neither you nor your spouse is covered by an employer's retirement plan, both can deduct up to $2,000.

✔ Contribute to a Roth IRA. The same deadline applies but the contribution is nondeductible and the requirements are different. On a joint return, you must have income under $150,000 to make a full $2,000-per-person contribution. After five years, as long as you're at least $59^{1}/_{2}$, all withdrawals will be tax-free.

✔ Contribute to a SEP. If you had self-employment income you can cut your taxes by setting up a simplified employee pension (SEP) plan. You can take deductions for the prior year as long as your contribution is made by the due date of the return, including extensions. Contributions are limited to roughly 13% of net self-employment income; the maximum contribution is $25,500. SEPs involve minimal paperwork.

✔ Avoid paperwork discrepancies. Make sure that all the income reported on the statements you receive from banks, brokers, mutual funds, and so on, is reflected on your tax return. The IRS devotes a tremendous amount of effort to document matching, so mismatching will draw unwelcome notice to your return.

✔ Remember reinvestments. When you determine the cost of securities you sold the previous year, be sure to include any amounts you previously reinvested, such as reinvested dividends and capital gains distributions from mutual funds. If you don't include them, you'll be paying tax twice on those reinvestments.

✔ Consider carryforwards. If you were unable to deduct all your capital losses in a previous year, see if you can use them to offset capital gains for the current year.

Similarly, if you were in a tax shelter that just wound up or if you sold rental property, you may be able to deduct all the accumulated but suspended losses.

✔ Take credit. If you invested in foreign stocks or foreign mutual funds, you probably had foreign taxes withheld. You can get a tax credit for such payments by filling out Form 1116, which is extremely convoluted. Since 1999, though, if your foreign tax was no more than $300 ($600 on a joint return), you can skip Form 1116 and claim the credit on your regular Form 1040.

With a little knowledge you can cast for investments around the world and keep your net gains from the tax collector's grasp.

Glossary

A trust a trust that makes income and principal available to a surviving spouse. Also known as a marital trust.

accommodator an unrelated party who holds the proceeds from a property sale while a tax-deferred exchange is completed.

acknowledged copy a signed and dated notice from a retirement plan custodian attesting to the receipt of a beneficiary designation.

acquisition indebtedness a loan secured by your house or by a vacation home, incurred when you build, buy, or substantially improve the property.

alternative minimum tax (AMT) a parallel tax system. Taxpayers pay whichever is higher, the regular tax or the AMT.

American Depositary Receipts (ADRs) investments that take the place of shares in foreign companies. ADRs trade in the United States on virtually the same terms as the shares of U.S. stocks.

AMT adjustments tax benefits that are added back to income when calculating an AMT obligation.

AMT munis tax-exempt bonds paying interest that is included in income, for AMT purposes.

annual gift tax exclusion tax benefit allowing gifts to be made, tax-free. Currently, each person can give away up to $10,000 per recipient per year.

asset-backed security a debt obligation in which the investor's return is due to come from specific contracts, such as a collection of car loans or credit-card loans.

asset protection trust a trust designed to preserve the assets from future creditors' claims.

B trust a trust in which assets are left to the next generation. Also known as a family trust.

bailout clause an escape hatch. If the rate on your fixed annuity drops by a certain amount, you can move your money to another company without owing any surrender charges.

balloon payment note a debt obligation that demands only interest payments until maturity.

bank letter of credit a document guaranteeing payment of a customer's obligations up to a stated amount for a given time period.

basis your basis in an asset is your cost for tax purposes.

basis point one-hundredth of a percent, or 0.01%.

basis step-up a tax break enjoyed by heirs to appreciated property. When you inherit an asset your basis is increased to its value at the owner's death, effectively eliminating the tax on all the gains that were not cashed in.

boot taxable profit from a transaction. In a tax-deferred real estate exchange, boot may be either cash proceeds or debt relief.

buy-sell agreement a contract spelling out the terms of business succession in case of death, retirement, or disability.

C corporation a business entity offering limited liability to shareholders. C corporations must pay a corporate income tax.

call feature the right, held by some bond issuers, to pay off bondholders before maturity, at a preset price.

carryforward a tax benefit that can't be used in one year so it is deferred to a future tax return.

cash balance plan a retirement plan that's actually a defined benefit (pension) plan but resembles a 401(k) plan to increase appeal to employees.

cash merger a transaction in which one company acquires another by offering money to shareholders.

cash-rich life insurance an insurance policy designed to build up a substantial investment account.

cash value the investment account in a permanent life insurance policy.

charitable lead trust (CLT) a trust that pays certain amounts to charity for a certain time period, then distributes the assets to individual beneficiaries.

charitable remainder trust (CRT) a trust that pays a specified amount to you or the other beneficiaries you name yet eventually will pass to a charity or charities you choose.

commissions compensation paid to a broker or other intermediary for arranging a securities trade.

country funds investment pools that invest in one particular foreign country.

covered option the obligation to sell a security you already own, on certain terms.

credit quality the likelihood that the issuer of a bond will live up to its obligations.

Crummey trust a trust accepting gifts that qualify for the annual gift tax exclusion. To do so, the beneficiaries must be given the right to withdraw these gifts.

custodial account an arrangement that permits minors to hold assets, which will become their property when they come of age.

custodian a financial institution that holds assets for investors. Those assets may be inside of a tax-deferred retirement plan.

customized beneficiary form a form prepared by a professional adviser detailing how an inherited retirement account is to be distributed.

deduction equivalent the amount of tax a deduction will save you, in a certain tax bracket. In the 36% bracket, for example, a $25,000 deduction saves $9,000 ($25,000 times 36% equals $9,000).

deemed liquidation tax trap that companies may fall into when switching from one business entity to another. Paper profits may be generated, leading to a tax obligation.

deferred annuity an investment in which you pay now, wait for many years, and then withdraw funds. Taxes on the investment buildup aren't due until the money is received.

defined benefit plan a tax-deferred retirement plan designed to pay a certain retirement benefit based on earnings and years of service.

defined contribution plan a tax-deferred retirement plan in which the ultimate payout depends on how well the contributed funds are invested.

depreciation a deduction for a noncash expense, the estimated wear and tear on property you own.

designated beneficiaries individuals or certain trusts named to inherit a retirement account.

dividends payments of profit by a corporation to its shareholders.

dynasty trust a trust designed to hold assets for the benefit of the creator's descendants.

economic benefit the value of insurance coverage obtained via a split dollar arrangement. This amount is taxable income to the covered employee.

education IRA an IRA that provides tax-free withdrawals if used to pay higher-education bills.

employee stock ownership plan (ESOP) a retirement plan in which ownership of a company is transferred to employees.

equities ownership interests. Publicly traded stocks are often called equities.

equity-indexed annuity fixed annuity in which your income is pegged to the performance of the stock market.

escrow an arrangement in which an unrelated third party holds money or other valuables until certain conditions are met.

family business and farm exclusion a tax benefit allowing a family business or farm to shelter more of its value from estate tax than would be the case with other types of assets.

family limited partnership (FLP) a partnership where senior family members usually act as general partners, in control of the assets. Ownership of those assets can be shifted to younger family members, who are limited partners.

fiduciary responsibility the obligation of a retirement plan sponsor or trustee to invest plan money wisely on behalf of all participants.

first mortgage a loan secured by real estate. The holder has the first claim on the property in case of a default.

fixed annuity a deferred annuity that promises to pay you an interest rate comparable to what you'd earn on a bond.

flexible spending account a fringe benefit offered by many employers. These plans permit employees to purchase goods and services with pretax rather than with after-tax dollars.

forfeitures funds in a retirement plan that are distributed among remaining participants when others leave before becoming fully vested.

401(k) plan a retirement plan in which employees elect to defer part of their salary. The deferred amounts are invested and no tax is due on the investment income until withdrawal.

general obligation (GO) bond a municipal bond that is backed by all of the issuer's resources, which makes the risk of default unlikely.

general partner a partner who does not enjoy limited liability and so is fully exposed to the partnership's obligations.

generation-skipping transfer trust a trust created to pass assets to grandchildren and even great-grandchildren while minimizing transfer taxes.

global funds investment pools that can invest anywhere in the world, including the United States.

Grandchildren's Incentive Trust a trust with provisions designed to motivate young beneficiaries to behave in a certain manner.

grantor trust a trust that generates income that's taxable to the trust creator rather than income reported on the trust's tax return.

growth fund a stock fund that buys companies with outstanding prospects for increasing earnings.

home equity indebtedness a loan secured by a home but used for purposes other than building, buying, or improving the house.

hybrid method a method that uses both the recalculation and term-certain method to provide both safety and extended tax deferral.

illiquid not easily sold at a market price.

immediate annuity a contract in which you give money to an insurance company, bank, or such, and get back an income stream that starts right away.

increasing death benefit option an insurance policy where the death benefit increases along with any increase in the policy's cash value.

index fund a mutual fund with a goal of matching a specified index rather than beating the market.

individual retirement account (IRA) earnings are not taxed, but the account must be emptied within a given time period and withdrawals are usually taxed.

insured bond an obligation that carries private insurance. In case the issuer is unable to repay investors, the obligation shifts to the insurance company.

in the money an option that has current value: either (1) a call where the exercise price is below the trading price or (2) a put where the exercise price is above the trading price.

investment income dividends, interest, and, in some cases, capital gains.

investment interest expense interest paid on loans taken out to make investments.

irrevocable trust a trust that cannot be canceled or significantly changed.

joint donor Wealth Trust a Wealth Trust funded by assets transferred from two spouses.

kiddie tax the tax code provision that treats some unearned income of children under 14 as being earned by their parents.

lapse expiration of a life insurance policy for lack of premium payments. In a permanent life policy, income taxes will be triggered.

large-caps stocks that have the greatest market capitalization; that is, their outstanding shares have the most value among publicly traded stocks. Generally, the most widely-known U.S. companies are large-caps.

leverage to use borrowed money to acquire assets such as real estate or securities.

limited liability company (LLC) a business entity combining the protection of a corporation with the tax planning opportunities of a partnership.

limited liability partnership (LLP) a business entity similar to an LLC, available to organizations such as professional service firms that may choose partnership status.

limited partner a partner who enjoys limited liability and makes no operating decisions.

limited partnership a partnership in which some parties enjoy protection from the venture's obligations.

liquid an asset is liquid if it is easily salable at a market price.

long-term capital gain profit from the sale of an asset held more than a year. Under current law, the maximum tax rate is 20%.

margin the amount an investor deposits with a broker when borrowing money from that broker. Margin can be in the form of cash or securities.

marginal tax rate the rate at which your last dollar (or your next dollar) of income will be taxed. Also known as your tax bracket.

margin call a demand from a broker to add more cash or securities to your margin deposit.

maturity the date when the issuer of a bond will repay bondholders a promised amount.

mid-caps stocks that are too big to be small-caps yet not sizable enough to be large-caps.

minimum distribution incidental benefit (MDIB) table schedule that increases required distributions, in many cases, when a young nonspouse is named as retirement plan beneficiary.

modified endowment contract (MEC) a life insurance policy bought with one large payment or several sizable payments. You aren't allowed tax-free loans or withdrawals from a MEC.

money purchase plan a type of defined contribution plan that requires employers to contribute certain amounts each year.

mortgage-backed security a debt obligation in which investors receive mortgage payments that have been made by property owners, usually homeowners.

municipal bond an obligation of a state or local government agency. The interest paid is generally exempt from federal income tax and perhaps from other income taxes as well.

naked option the obligation to sell a security you don't own. If you have to sell it you'll have to buy it first, at any price, so your potential loss is enormous.

negative election 401(k) a retirement plan design that calls for all eligible employees to participate in a 401(k) plan unless they expressly choose not to do so.

net unrealized appreciation (NUA) paper profits on company stock withdrawn from a tax-deferred retirement plan. Eventually, a sale of this stock may qualify for favorable long-term capital gains treatment.

nondiscrimination test calculation designed to ensure that an employer-sponsored retirement plan benefits most employees, not just top management.

ordinary income taxable income that receives no favorable tax treatment.

out of the money an option with no current value.

overfunded plan a defined benefit plan that currently holds assets greater than those needed to make the required payments. At this point, further contributions are not permitted.

participating mortgage a loan that entitles the lender to a share in any future property appreciation, in addition to interest.

partnership an unincorporated business with two or more principals. The opportunity to allocate income among partners leads to planning opportunities.

passive losses real or paper losses from investment property or from an active business in which you don't participate. In many cases, such losses are not deductible right away.

permanent life insurance a policy that calls for relatively high initial premiums in order to keep the insurance in force as you grow older.

personal access version Wealth Trust a Wealth Trust funded by only one spouse, who may name the other spouse as trustee and beneficiary.

policy illustration computer-generated projection showing how a permanent life insurance policy may perform in the future.

positive cash flow revenues from a venture such as rental real estate that exceed the out-of-pocket costs.

premium payment for an insurance policy.

prepaid premium account an arrangement in which an employer makes some split dollar payments in advance.

private family foundation a charitable entity established to allow the creator and successors to control future donations.

private letter ruling an IRS decision that applies to one particular tax-payer's situation, not meant to serve as a general precedent.

probate the process of proving a will, which may be expensive and time-consuming.

profit-sharing plan a type of defined contribution plan in which employers can contribute varying amounts each year.

prohibited transactions investment activities forbidden to fiduciaries.

property option the right to acquire real estate during a certain time at a specified price.

protected retirement account a strategy that calls for a trust to buy a cash-value life insurance policy that can be tapped for tax-free retirement income.

prototype plans easy-to-use retirement plans provided to employers by trust companies, brokers, mutual fund companies, and insurers.

provisional income an amount derived to determine if Social Security benefits will be taxable. To calculate provisional income you add your adjusted gross income, your tax-exempt interest income, and one-half of your Social Security benefits.

prudent investor guidelines requirements that a fiduciary must invest with the entire portfolio in mind, taking reasonable risks in order to achieve substantial returns.

qualified personal residence trust (QPRT) a trust used to pass a residence to the next generation at a low gift-tax value.

qualified state tuition plan program that provides tax deferral and tax-bracket reduction to encourage investing for higher education.

qualified terminable interest property (QTIP) trust a trust from which the surviving spouse receives all the income, yet the trust fund ultimately goes to beneficiaries named by the first spouse to die.

recalculation method a method of withdrawing retirement plan money that extends the recipients' life expectancy each year.

recapture payback for previous depreciation deductions. When you sell depreciated property, your taxable gain will include depreciation that you've deducted in the past.

refinance replace an old mortgage with a new (presumably less expensive) mortgage.

required beginning date the date when retirement plan withdrawals must begin, April 1 of the next year after you reach $70\frac{1}{2}$.

required minimum distribution amount that must be withdrawn from a tax-deferred retirement plan after age $70\frac{1}{2}$ upon pain of a 50% penalty tax.

revenue bond a municipal bond backed by the proceeds from a specific project, which means there is some risk investors won't be repaid.

revenue ruling an IRS announcement that is meant to indicate the agency's official stance on a tax issue.

reverse mortgage a loan secured by a house that's fully paid for or carries little debt. The homeowner can use the cash flow, deferring repayment.

reverse split dollar a split dollar arrangement in which the employee owns the policy but the company is named the beneficiary for a portion of the death benefit.

Roth IRA an IRA that offers no deductions for contributions but which may provide tax-free withdrawals after five years and age $59\frac{1}{2}$.

Roth IRA conversion change of a regular IRA to a Roth IRA, which triggers an obligation to pay the deferred income tax.

S corporation a business entity offering the liability protection of a corporation without the need to pay the corporate income tax. Any corporate profits are taxed to the shareholders as personal income.

secondary market a formal or informal network where securities that already have been issued may be bought and sold.

second mortgage in case of default, lenders who make second mortgage loans can collect only after the holder of the first mortgage is paid in full.

second-to-die life insurance a policy that pays off after the deaths of two people, usually a married couple.

Securities and Exchange Commission (SEC) the federal agency that regulates trading in stocks, bonds, mutual funds, and so on.

self-dealing transactions between the owner of an IRA or another tax-deferred retirement plan and parties connected by kinship or business association.

self-directed plans company-sponsored retirement plans that let employees make their own investment decisions with their personal accounts.

shrinking trust strategy a plan calling for a surviving spouse to spend one's own assets and those of own trust fund so that the children's trust fund (exempt from estate tax) can grow substantially.

SIMPLE plan a low-paperwork retirement plan (savings incentive match plan for employees) available to employers with no more than 100 employees.

simplified employee pension (SEP) a tax-deferred retirement plan requiring little paperwork.

small-caps publicly traded stocks with relatively small market values. (Notice the word "relatively"—some small-caps have market values up to $1 billion.)

sole proprietorship an unincorporated business run by a single individual.

split dollar life insurance an arrangement in which an employer pays some or all of the premiums for insuring the life of an employee.

sponsor person or company organizing a venture such as an investment partnership. In another context, an employer who offers a retirement plan to employees.

stock merger a transaction in which the shareholders in the target company receive shares of stock in the acquiring company.

stock options the rights to acquire common stock at a given price during a preset time period.

street name the practice of having securities held by your broker rather than keeping the certificates yourself.

stretch-out IRA an IRA that extends tax-free compounding to the children and perhaps even the grandchildren of the original owner.

strike price the price at which an option can be exercised.

subaccounts investment accounts inside a variable annuity, a variable MEC, or a variable life insurance policy.

substantially equal periodic payments (SEPPs) withdrawals from a tax-deferred retirement plan based on life expectancy. If these payments last at least five years and past age $59^1/_2$, there will be no 10% penalty for early withdrawals.

super-freeze a sophisticated estate planning strategy designed to remove future asset appreciation from someone's estate.

surrender charge payment you owe to an annuity issuer if you withdraw too much, too soon.

tax-adjusted return a mutual fund's total return, after certain assumptions for an investor's tax obligations are taken into account.

tax credit a direct reduction of a tax obligation.

tax-deferred exchange a transaction in which one investment property is replaced with another while no income taxes are paid.

term-certain method a retirement plan withdrawal method that fixes a time period.

term life insurance pure life insurance, without an investment account.

term-of-years foundation a private foundation that will make charitable contributions for a set time period, after which the principal will pass to designated individuals.

third mortgage holders of third mortgages come after the holders of first and second mortgages if a borrower defaults.

total return an investment's income return (interest, dividends) for a given time period plus or minus price appreciation or depreciation, realized or not.

trust grantor the person who creates and funds a trust.

turnover rate a measure of how actively a mutual fund trades its holdings. A fund with a 100% turnover rate holds each investment for an average of one year before selling it.

unified transfer credit an offset against gift and estate tax. Each individual's credit shelters $675,000 worth of tax in 2000, an amount that will rise gradually to $1 million in 2006.

unit investment trusts (UITs) an investment vehicle that pools money from many investors and buys a fixed portfolio of stocks and bonds. Investors' shares are called units.

universal life insurance (UL) permanent life insurance that offers flexibility in premium payments.

unlimited marital deduction tax benefit allowing one spouse to give or bequeath any amount to the other spouse, tax-free.

valuation discount a reduction in the expressed value of an asset transferred to a family member, who lacks control over that asset. Such discounts may save gift or estate tax.

value fund a mutual fund that specializes in buying stocks that seem low-priced compared to the overall market.

variable annuity a deferred annuity that allows you to direct your investment into various accounts, including stock funds.

variable life insurance permanent life insurance that offers investors the chance to direct premiums into stock funds, bond funds, and so on.

vesting the process in which employees must work for a company for a certain length of time before they're eligible to receive retirement benefits.

whole life insurance permanent life insurance with level premiums and a level death benefit.

wrap programs arrangements in which investors pay fees rather than sales commissions for investment advice. Typically, the fee paid is a percentage of the value of the assets in the account.

yield the periodic cash return on an investment: interest on a bond or a dividend on a stock.

Index